Cambridge Elements

Elements in the Gothic
edited by
Dale Townshend
Manchester Metropolitan University
Angela Wright
University of Sheffield

AFRICAN AMERICAN GOTHIC IN THE ERA OF BLACK LIVES MATTER

Maisha Wester
Indiana University

CAMBRIDGE
UNIVERSITY PRESS

Shaftesbury Road, Cambridge CB2 8EA, United Kingdom

One Liberty Plaza, 20th Floor, New York, NY 10006, USA

477 Williamstown Road, Port Melbourne, VIC 3207, Australia

314–321, 3rd Floor, Plot 3, Splendor Forum, Jasola District Centre, New Delhi – 110025, India

103 Penang Road, #05-06/07, Visioncrest Commercial, Singapore 238467

Cambridge University Press is part of Cambridge University Press & Assessment, a department of the University of Cambridge.

We share the University's mission to contribute to society through the pursuit of education, learning and research at the highest international levels of excellence.

www.cambridge.org
Information on this title: www.cambridge.org/9781009571401

DOI: 10.1017/9781009161008

© Maisha Wester 2025

This publication is in copyright. Subject to statutory exception and to the provisions of relevant collective licensing agreements, no reproduction of any part may take place without the written permission of Cambridge University Press & Assessment.

When citing this work, please include a reference to the DOI 10.1017/9781009161008

First published 2025

A catalogue record for this publication is available from the British Library

ISBN 978-1-009-57140-1 Hardback
ISBN 978-1-009-16101-5 Paperback
ISSN 2634-8721 (online)
ISSN 2634-8713 (print)

Additional resources for this publication at www.cambridge.org/Wester

Cambridge University Press & Assessment has no responsibility for the persistence or accuracy of URLs for external or third-party internet websites referred to in this publication and does not guarantee that any content on such websites is, or will remain, accurate or appropriate.

African American Gothic in the Era of Black Lives Matter

Elements in the Gothic

DOI: 10.1017/9781009161008
First published online: January 2025

Maisha Wester
Indiana University

Author for correspondence: Maisha Wester, maisha.wester@sheffield.ac.uk

Abstract: This Element explores twenty-first century Black Gothic literature and film as it responds to American anti-Blackness and as they illustrate a mode of Black Gothic fiction termed Black Lives Matter (BLM) Gothic. The various texts express frustration, rage, and sorrow over the failures of previous civil rights fights. Intended as an introduction to a complex mode, this Element explores the three central themes in BLM Gothic texts and defines the mode's pattern of tropes. The first section reviews the depictions of American anti-Blackness, and defines the mode's pattern of tropes reveal the necropolitical mechanisms at play in US systemic racism. The second section explores the ways the fictions 'make whiteness strange' in order to destabilize white normativity and shatter the power arising from such claims. The final section examines the costs of waging war against racial oppression and the power of embracing 'monstrosity'.

Keywords: Black Lives Matter, racism, Black Horror, Black Gothic, race theory

© Maisha Wester 2025

ISBNs: 9781009571401 (HB), 9781009161015 (PB), 9781009161008 (OC)
ISSNs: 2634-8721 (online), 2634-8713 (print)

Contents

Introduction: Say The(ir) Name(s)   1

1 You Already Dead   9

2 Making Whiteness Strange   30

3 Becoming the Monster   48

Conclusion: When Tomorrow Comes   65

Bibliography   72

Introduction: Say The(ir) Name(s)

> You can be shot and killed while in the presence of your child (as in the cases of Philando Castile and Korryn Gaines), while running or walking away from police (as with Walter Scott and Rekia Boyd), while playing with a toy gun in an open-carry state (as with Tamir Rice and John Crawford), or even while in police custody (as with Sandra Bland and Freddie Gray).[1]
>
> Candyman is a way to deal with the fact that these things happened to us. Are still happening![2]

On 7 September 2017 Glynn Washington debuted his podcast series *Spooked* as a side project to the radio series *Snap Judgement*, a show addressing issues of social disenfranchisement. On the surface, *Spooked* is a collection of stories of ghostly encounters told by the people who experienced them. Washington begins each episode with a brief introduction alluding to the stories' focal events and/or terrors. In the second season, Washington's introductions began featuring real stories of racial horror. These introductions elide the usual sense of supernatural encounter, focusing instead on the mundane terrors and traumas of Black existence in America. For example, Washington begins the episode 'Dismal Falls' with the story of Detroit's Devil's Night provided in audio clip 1.

Audio 1 Introduction to 'Dismal Falls' by *Spooked* Audio file available at www.cambridge.org/Wester

Source: *Spooked*, Snap Judgement. Available online at https://spookedpodcast.org/

Unlike the central story, Devil's Night has nothing to do with spiritual, disembodied beings. Rather, the story recounts his grandfather's experience of anti-Black violence, told as he keeps watch on their porch with a shotgun in his lap.[3] Washington begins another episode, 'The Intruders', by recounting his introduction to sexualized racist aggression. In audio clip 2, Washington recalls witnessing a white handyman sexually proposition his mother in exchange for reduced service fees.

Audio 2 Introduction to "The Intruders" by *Spooked* Audio file available at www.cambridge.org/Wester

Source: *Spooked*, Snap Judgment. Available online at https://spookedpodcast.org/episode-214-the-intruders

---

[1] Hitchens, 'Contextualizing Police', pp. 434–438.
[2] *Candyman,* directed by Nia DaCosta (Monkeypaw, 2021), film.
[3] Washington, 'Dismal Falls'.

Little Washington steps out into the hallway, surprising the man, and walks past the two into the kitchen where he retrieves a butter-knife,

> will[ing] it to be sharper ... and I will stab this red-headed man with it. ... I know I will kill this person. I'd just been drinking a glass of milk, watching *The Flintstones* but I know with utter certainty that I will kill him or perish in the process. Almost as if it has already happened, I know it. ... Maybe he's already decided to take his leave. Or maybe he sees the cold rage in a nine-year old boy's eyes. He places his cap back on his head, nods to my mother, and backs out the front door.[4]

Even after the man left and Washington returned to watching cartoons, his rage refuses to subside but instead builds and he imagines various ways of killing the red-headed man. Washington concludes, wondering 'if in another world there's another me sitting in his room, not clenched, not furious, sitting in the same chair after washing the blood from a butter-knife'.[5]

As a series focusing on tales of the other-worldly, *Spooked* is part of a global trend. Unlike many other Horror and Haunting podcasts, Washington sporadically peppers his racial history introductions throughout the episodes; it is the one horror he returns to, unlike the central narratives of the featured storytellers. Like racial violence itself, these narratives appear without warning. *Spooked* is distinct in situating white supremacy and anti-Black violence as chief among its horrors. It shudders at the 'myriad minute decisions that constitute the practices of the world [which] are at every point informed by judgements about people's capacities and worth, judgements based on what they look like, where they come from, how they speak, even what they eat, that is, racial judgements'.[6] This violent and violating anti-Blackness haunts because of its consistent return across different eras and generations. Furthermore, the irregularity of the introductions focusing on the history of violent anti-Blackness means that the series avoids the problem of reductionist and/or exploitative rhetoric; it evades being dismissed as 'Black Trauma Porn'. Washington's strategic deployment of the narratives essentially argues that while race is not the sole factor governing the horrors of the United States, 'it is never not a factor, never not in play'.[7] Unlike the 'spooks' of the shows' storytellers, anti-Blackness horrifies because it is very much alive when it should have been long dead.

Though *Spooked* is exceptional as a podcast for its racial interventions into the narratives of haunting and terror which have become trendy, it is not exceptional in its place in Black Gothic and Horror Fiction. *Spooked* follows

---

[4] Washington, 'The Intruders'.
[5] Washington, 'The Intruders'. In many ways this narrative recalls Frederick Douglass's experience in seeing his Aunt Hester whipped.
[6] Dyer, *White*, p. 1.   [7] Dyer, *White*, p. 1.

the trend set by films such as *Two Distant Strangers* (2020) and *Candyman* (2021), series like *Lovecraft Country* (2020) and *Them* (2021), and fiction such as *Ghost Boys* by Jewell Parker Rhodes and *Victor LaValle's Destroyer* by Victor LaValle in a new mode of African American Gothic which reiterates the impetus, hope, and despair of the Black Lives Matter (BLM) movement.[8] Black Lives Matter (BLM) Gothic, as I term this latest vein of African American Gothic, centres upon a racially targeted violence that defies rational explanation. The fictions build upon ideas of haunting begun in canonical African American Gothic texts like *Beloved* in which the ghost is the least of the terrors witnessed throughout the story. Yet unlike Toni Morrison's text, BLM Gothic offers no remedy or even partial solution and denies the certainty of progress. The horror does not wait in the distance to return in the wake of forgetfulness. Rather, in BLM Gothic racist violence remains an ever-present, vile poltergeist that defies immediate remedy.

Founded by three black women, BLM as a movement gained momentum as extrajudicial murders of Black people became increasingly visible, and as an explicitly anti-Black, anti-immigrant misogynist won the Republican presidential nomination. Invested in social justice, BLM fights for a liberated Black future by recording and protesting the racial horrors of the present. Yet as Gothic texts such as Childish Gambino's 'This is America' suggests, the methods of BLM resistance may prove ultimately ineffective. Thus the same brutal shifts of the early twenty-first century which necessitated BLM also impacted the trajectory of African American literature towards Afropessimism, a theory which contends that Black people have never accessed the status of 'Human' but remain Slaves, perpetual (social) corpses buried beneath (and thus bolstering) white societies. The theory argues anti-Blackness is essential to the psychic health of all non-Blacks; consequently, Black people remain non-subjects in relation to the world. In insisting that civil society – indeed the very notion of the 'Human' – is structured upon the violent exclusion of Blacks to the place of commodified nonbeings, Afropessimism is an inherently Gothic project. And BLM Gothic and Horror is intrinsically Afropessimistic.

As I have noted elsewhere, using the Gothic and Horror genres to express the nightmarish reality and consequences of racism in US sociopolitics is a difficult project. Gothic fiction and Horror film have long played host to problematic racial ideologies, have provided oppressive political discourses with a plethora of tropes to dehumanize African Americans, and have proven integral in 'set-[ting] the standards of humanity by which they [white people] are bound to

---

[8] The BLM movement began in July 2013 after George Zimmerman was acquitted for the shooting death of seventeen-year-old Trayvon Martin. The BLM started as the hashtag BlackLivesMatter.

succeed and others bound to fail'.[9] Frantz Fanon, in clarifying the European imago of Black people, explains that 'In this imaginary economy, the Negro is not a human but an object. More exactly, the Negro is a phobic object that, as such, arouses fear and terror'.[10] In other words, the project of racial construction is itself inherently a Gothic/Horror project. Unsurprisingly, assailants often turn to the language of monstrosity to recount their encounters with their Black victims. Darren Wilson, the officer who shot Michael Brown, described his victim as having 'the most aggressive face. . . . it looks like a demon, that's how angry he looked'.[11] Similarly '[Eleanor] Bumpurs was depicted as a "mad black woman" and "looming monstrosity" whose race, overweight appearance, and history of mental illness were used as rationale for police use of excessive force – even while nude and in the privacy of her home'.[12] As the shooting of twelve-year-old Tamir Rice[13] and attempted arrests of other Black pre-teens show, even children are targets of a racial ideology and system that sees Blacks as monstrous.

Yet the Gothic's insistence that we are far from the civilized, enlightened societies that we imagine ourselves to be render it highly effective as a vehicle for BLM Gothic and Horror. Although the language of monstrosity has traditionally been turned against people of colour, such populations do successfully mobilize the tropes to point back at the originators. The Gothic trope of haunting is indispensable to BLM Gothic and Horror, as previously noted. However, the form of haunting in BLM Gothic differs from that in earlier Black Gothic literature, as Sheri-Marie Harrison explains in her definition of the New Black Gothic, in which BLM Gothic participates:

> unlike in, say, Morrison's *Beloved*, the spectral reappearance of America's violent history in recent fiction is neither about recovery nor representation. . . . . Instead, racial violence has never gone away. It is indeed, as the ghosts are, at home with us. . . . ghosts speak to an ever-present and visible lineage of violence that accumulates rather than dissipates with the passage of time. Gothic violence remains a part of everyday black life.[14]

Notably, Harrison's definition of the New Black Gothic also situates it within Afropessimism given the accumulative nature of the violence. Such works eschew 'liberatory *telos*. . . in favor of a much less programmatic relationship to the meaning of history and to the potentiality of black futurity' [italic in the original] and 'bear the marks of what Erica Edwards has called "the new black novel as . . . devastated form"'.[15]

---

[9] Dyer, *White*, p. 9. [10] Mbembe, *Necropolitics*, p. 138.
[11] Bouie, 'Michael Brown Wasn't a Superhuman Demon'.
[12] Hitchens, 'Contextualizing Police', p. 436.
[13] Rice's murder haunts BLM Gothic texts as a number of Black children are aged twelve-years old.
[14] Harrison, 'New Black Gothic'. [15] Jenkins, 'Afro-Futurism/Afro-Pessimism', p. 129.

BLM Gothic texts, in refuting the notion of racial violence as a distant phenomenon that ripples into the present, rely upon reproducing scenes from recent events and history to produce Real Horror rather than imagined terrors. As Robert C Solomon notes, unlike Art Horror, Real Horror denies us satisfaction and pleasure. Real Horror is that which is truly horrible and 'renders the subject/victim helpless and violates his or her most rudimentary expectations about the world'.[16] Real Horror arises unbidden and haunts in the seeming randomness of its occurrence. BLM Gothic, through its reliance upon real-life events and encounters, pushes readers and audiences to acknowledge 'that things are not as they ought to be or not as one thought they were'[17] in a post-Civil Rights era, twenty-first-century nation. In doing so, BLM Gothic 'paralyze[s] and dumbfound[s] as people struggle to understand how something so unthinkable, so beyond any expectations, could come to pass'.[18]

One of the consequences of this paralyzing awareness of the horrific state of affairs is a refusal to provide anything like a happy-ending. Rather, the fictions iterate 'a sense of inescapability and the eschewal of hope for the future. These contemporary black Gothic texts bring into sharp focus the near-constant vulnerability of black life'.[19] Yet, as a social justice movement, BLM is inherently hopeful. Black Lives Matter envisions a liberated future 'where Black people across the diaspora thrive, experience joy, and are not defined by their struggles. ... a future fully divested from police, prisons, and all punishment paradigms and which invests in justice, joy, and culture'. However as much as the movement is hopeful in its goals, Black witnessing and activism is not without consequence. BLM Gothic is in part a testament to the casualties of BLM activism: young activists and organizers like Edward Crawford, Erica Garner, and Cheslie Kryst who have died from heart failure and suicide. As BLM organizer and activist Ashley Yates explains, 'I have to make clear just how invisible some of the most heinous violence we experience is . . . . How we are often left alone on the front lines grown cold because media and figureheads move on to the next hot story'.[20] Deaths like Marshawn McCarrel's suggest that the terrible sociopolitical reality may outweigh the activists' hope.[21]

Thus BLM Gothic is rooted in a racial pessimism arising from confronting 'white America's deep belief and conviction that the freedom and security of the white race can be guaranteed only at the expense of the life of nonwhites, even if

---

[16] Solomon, *In Defense*, p. 119.   [17] Solomon, *In Defense*, p. 60.
[18] Benson-Allott, 'Learning from Horror', p. 61.   [19] Harrison, 'New Black Gothic'.
[20] Eligon, 'The Quiet Casualties of the Movement for Black Lives'.
[21] McCarrel, another BLM activist and organizer, committed suicide on the steps of the Ohio State House in February of 2016.

this prospect might lead to catastrophe'.[22] The fiction articulates the notion implicit in the anti-Black violence which necessitated the BLM movement; that

> for white America to exist at all, it must continuously produce a complex of bodies in chains (Niggers). "Niggers" are not only the condition of possibility of America; they are also a class of people America cannot live with, people America doesn't want to share anything with, although without them America means nothing or not much. America, in this sense, means the impossibility of sharing freedom with others.[23]

Such racial pessimism results in endings which are mere pauses in the nightmare, not actual escapes. Significantly, this denial of hope reflects back to the unhappy unendings which predominated early Gothic texts such as *Frankenstein* (1818). It is also part of an aesthetic which 'represent[s] black life on its own terrorized terms',[24] refuting ideologies of inherent Black monstrosity even as the envisioned solutions to anti-Black violence are themselves problematic stopgaps. History is horrible, BLM Gothic notes, but the present is as bad if not worse.

BLM Gothic's tropes reproduce traditional Gothic tropes with some important variations. As in traditional texts, the hero(in)es are often isolated (see e.g. *Two Distant Strangers*, Victor LaValle's *Destroyer*, *Ghost Boys*, and 'Haint in the Window') or are part of a small, isolated group (see e.g. *Them*, *Lovecraft Country*, and *The First Purge*). The hero(in)es are isolated only in a metaphorical sense, as they often find themselves amidst a sea of alienating white Americans. Thus Carter, the hero of *Two Distant Strangers,* is repeatedly attacked and murdered on one of New York City's bustling sidewalks. Police harass Tommy in the middle of Harlem and Red Hook in *The Ballad of Black Tom*. The opening sequence of *Get Out* exemplifies this trope as Andre wanders through a well-lit and white-populated suburb; the whiteness of the locale, emphasized in the streets lined with white houses, is the source of Andre's terror in which he is isolated as a lone Black man walking, he notes, through a hedge maze. Chris explicitly defines this sense of isolation amongst a sea of people, declaring 'sometimes, when there's too many white people, I get nervous'.

In terms of settings, the texts are largely based in real, recognizable locations across the United States. *Them* takes place in Oakland, California; *The First Purge* occurs in Staten Island; and *Destroyer* occurs in various locations across the United States, from Maryland to South Dakota. The choice to set these narratives in actual locales stresses the uncanniness of the US landscape for Blacks. Furthermore, in refusing to limit the violence to imagined and/or southern spaces, the fictions emphasize that the blood tide of racial oppression and violence mars the entire

---

[22] Mmembe, *Necropolitics*, p. 162. [23] Mmembe, *Necropolitics*, p. 162.
[24] Harrison, 'New Black Gothic'.

nation. Consequently, while the film short 'Everybody Dies!' (2016)[25] is set in the underworld, the Grim Reaper frequently refers to a map of the United States with lights across the country.

The villains of BLM Gothic are, unsurprisingly, white Americans. These monstrous antagonists are always part of a larger system of racial oppression and violence. Rhodes's novel *Ghost Boys* best exemplifies this trend. Taking place in the aftermath of the police-shooting twelve-year-old Jerome, the child-ghost witnesses not only the officer's trial and acquittal, but sees for the first time the relative luxury that is the white Chicago suburbs and school system. In contrast, a lack of resources and excessive violence disfigure Jerome's predominantly Black school district and neighbourhood. The juxtaposition of the officer's trial with Jerome's exploration of the suburban library, parks, and resplendent homes signifies the white officer's violence as part of a larger system of oppression that dooms Blacks. Similarly, the violent assailants in *The First Purge* are all white men, with the exception of Skeletor who is effectively weaponized by a white scientist. Yet both Skeletor and the militia serve the agenda of the leading political group, The Founding Fathers, which organized the Purge and targeted the Black location.

The villains in these films typically assume a degree of obscene, but very human, monstrosity. The texts repeatedly render white antagonists grotesque figures through their rejection of basic 'human' principles. As such BLM Gothic participates in that 'cultural shift [which] aligns monstrosity not with physical difference, but with antithetical moral values'.[26] The climax of *Two Distant Strangers*, for instance, is the revelation of Officer Merks' monstrosity as he applauds Carter's attempt to enlighten Merk in negotiating for his life. The film slows down in the moment before Merk shoots Carter yet again, focusing on the single, shining gold tooth in Merks' twisted mouth. Other scenes see Merks' face contorted as he variously strangles and kills Carter with his bare hands. Similarly, *Them* relies on the increasingly terrifying violence of the white neighbours for its monstrosity. Yet the fictions also render white villains physically monstrous; the perpetrators in *The First Purge* sometimes blend their historical attire, such as KKK robes and SS-officer uniforms, with terrifying masks. Similarly, though Christina Braithwhite largely retains her spotless fashion throughout *Lovecraft Country*,[27] her male counterpart – Officer Seamus Lancaster – is literally a patchwork of parts stolen from the bodies of his Black victims. Lastly, any other monstrous supernatural creatures that appear in the

---

[25] 'Everybody Dies!', directed by Nuotama Bodomo, in *Collective: Unconscious* (Flies Collective and EAMS, 2016), film.
[26] Weinstock, 'Invisible Monsters', p. 276.
[27] The crisp, sharp lines of Christina's attire serve to make her appear more mechanical than human. The series' costume designer Pink explicitly noted that her goal was to convey a sharpness and edge to Christina: 'I want you to not want to touch her'. 'A Breakdown of Lovecraft Country's Costumes'.

texts function as tools of white oppression and systemic violence. This is especially true of *Lovecraft Country* which sees white Cthulhus[28] attacking the heroes. In all of these cases, moral and physical monstrosity serve to destabilize an especially abhorrent aspect of white systemic dominance: the 'assumption that white people are just people, which is not far off saying that whites are people whereas other colours are something else'.[29] BLM Gothic repeatedly reminds us that, through embracing such amoral dominance and violence, whites themselves become some 'thing' else and the humanity whiteness signifies inherently abhuman.

In response to horrifying encounters which are supported by systemic racism, the hero(in)es of these texts eventually defend themselves by embracing the violence they initially eschewed. In each fiction, non-violent protagonist weather repeated psychological violence and microaggressions with little more than an uncomfortable sigh. Confrontations with extreme physical violence forces each to access a degree of monstrosity in order to survive. Chris finally fights his way out of the house in *Get Out* after enduring a weekend of microaggressions, Nya the peaceful activist in *The First Purge* helps stage a siege on the militia, Akai must rip Frankenstein's Creature – the only other being like Akai – apart in *Destroyer*, and Anthony becomes Candyman and kills several white officers to protect his former lover in *Candyman* (2022). This repeated pattern alludes both to the rationale for non-violence and its failures. More horrifying is the way this defence slips into the terrain of monstrosity. As such, BLM Gothic hero(in)es have something in common with the Final Girl figure defined in Carol J. Clover's overview of Slasher films in *Men, Women, and Chainsaws*. For Clover, part of the horror of the Slasher film was this slippage into monstrosity by a figure that began as virtuous. This too is part of the horrified (un)endings of BLM Gothic. Such monstrous turns also reiterate the mode's Afropessimist grounding, given Afropessimism's inclination towards 'destroying worlds',[30] as well as the theory's horror at its truths; as Wilderson explains: 'I believe that the way out is a kind of violence so magnificent and so comprehensive that it scares the hell out of even radical revolutionaries'.[31]

As noted earlier, sociopolitical history and resistance methodologies inform BLM Gothic's revision of traditional Gothic and Horror tropes. To that end, this Element will introduce you to three of the central tenants of the new trend. Section 1 provides an overview of racist necropolitics as they appear and function in reality and in the fiction. The section considers BLM Gothic's depiction of Blacks as necropolitical objects and their consequent exile from citizenship; Blacks in the texts are metaphorical zombies, living but socio-politically dead. In each case, the texts reveal how

---

[28] Atticus manages to create a Cthulhu of his own but this creature is noticeably darker and appears only to protect the Black heroes. The creature never initiates violence, unlike the white Cthulhus.
[29] Dyer, *White*, p. 2.   [30] Jenkins, 'Afro-Futurism/Afro-Pessimism', p. 128.
[31] Qtd in Jenkins, 'Afro-Futurism/Afro-Pessimism', p. 128.

Black existence in America is inherently Gothic as Blacks remain targeted for consumption and disposal in the service of whiteness.

Section 2 focuses on how the texts attempt to destabilize whiteness to 'make it strange'. The section considers how BLM Gothic takes up Richard Dyer's contention that the only way to end white supremacy is by de-normalizing it, thereby making whiteness and its power mechanisms visible. In doing so, BLM Gothic also reveals how whiteness corrupts and infects non-white spaces and populations, rendering intracommunal spaces and populations nightmarish. Yet even so, the texts insist that such created nightmares are still far less terrifying and alienating than predominantly white locations. As such, the texts destabilize the idea of white normativity, depicting it as a mask for cannibalistic grotesquery.

Section 3 considers the problem of self-defence and survival in BLM Gothic texts. The mode is marked by unhappy (un)endings in part because the protagonists must accede to a level of monstrosity in defending their lives. Hero(in)es in BLM Gothic grapple with the question of defying and embracing stereotypes in the midst of resisting anti-Black violence. The section meditates on the question BLM Gothic poses: what does it mean or matter if you're called a monster by a horrifying society in the business of making people monstrous?

This is by no means a complete overview of BLM Gothic. There is much more to say about the numerous other issues at play in BLM Gothic texts, such as questions around the power of witnessing, the horror of intracommunal violence, and the nature of interracial allyship. Similarly, this Element limits the BLM Gothic texts covered in its overview. This study examines the novels and novellas *Ghost Boys* (Jewelle Parker Rhodes), *The Ballad of Black Tom* (Victor LaValle), and *Victor LaValle's Destroyer*; the short story 'Haint in the Window' (Tananarive Due); the films 'Everybody Dies!' (2016), *Get Out* (2017), and *Candyman* (2021); and the television series *Lovecraft Country* (2020). While these texts are exemplary, there are many more which fall under the purview of this study. The texts under discussion here were chosen based on their popularity, their creators' standing in Black Gothic, and the social debates they engendered. Lastly, while there are certainly BLM Gothic texts which appear outside of the US context, diasporic films like *His House* (2020), *Saloum* (2022) and novels like *The Girl With All the Gifts* (2014) – while similarly targeted in their ideological concern – do not abide by the same conventions as those deployed in the American context. This Element is merely an introduction to a rich and complex vein of US Black Gothic.

1 You Already Dead

Let me paint a picture of what's waiting for you on the shore. You all get to be slaves. Split up, sold off and worked to death. The lucky ones get Sunday off to sleep and fuck and make mo' slaves and all for what? For cotton? Indigo? For a Fucking purple shirt? .... A hundred year later, you're fucked. A hundred years after that ... .fucked. A hundred years after that, you get free, you still gettin' fucked outta' jobs and shot at by police. .... You are staring down the barrel of 300 years of subjugation, racist bullshit, and heart disease.[32]

Who do you think makes the hood? The city cuts off the community and waits for it to die. Then they invite developers in and say "Hey, you artists, you young people, you white, preferably or only, please come to the hood, its cheap. And if you stick it out for a couple for years, we'll bring you a Whole Foods.[33]

He didn't see you. My father didn't really see you.[34]

To behold a slave ship is to behold a floating cemetery. The belly of the slave ship reproduced the climate of the coffin, and the first lesson for the enslaved was to see themselves as 'already dead'. But, as Anansi's speech explains in the first epigraph, the end of slavery did not bring life and liberty for Black subjects. Rather the US sociopolitical system traps them within an invisible coffin. As *Candyman*'s description of gentrification clarifies, Black populations are figuratively offered up as sacrifices to white consumption well before their actual demise. Caught in a seemingly endless cycle of subjugation, violence, and disenfranchisement, Black Americans confront the nightmare of their living deaths.

Anansi's speech appears as part of *American Gods*, a series devoted to exploring the creation of the United States, alongside its sociopolitics, beliefs, and desires – in short, its 'gods'. Anansi gives this speech in the second episode of the series; the first episode featured a failed Viking conquest. The juxtaposition implies that the United States would have proven a failed conquest were it not for its enslaved population. The series, devoted to re-imagining the ideals of a country that proclaims freedom for and equality among men in its founding document, reminds viewers of the unsettling truth of the United States: its democracy was and remains dependent upon the disenfranchisement and dehumanization of a portion of its people. US democracy is doomed to bifurcation, characterized by

> a community of fellow creatures governed, at least in principle, by the law of equality, and a category of nonfellows, or even of those without part, that is also established by law. A priori, those without part have no right to have rights. They are governed by the law of inequality .... [thus] enabl[ing] a practically unbridgeable distance to be upheld between the community of fellow creatures and its others.[35]

Consequently, emancipation merely brought a new form of slavery, in many states quite literally, as generations of Black people remain damned to 'a poisoned heritage' in which the state of baseness and ignominy hardly changed

---

[32] *American Gods*, 'The Secret of Spoons', Amazon Prime, 7 May 2017, series.
[33] *Candyman* (2021). [34] Rhodes, *Ghost Boys*, p. 190. [35] Mbembe, *Necropolitics*, p. 17.

for the vast majority.[36] This is the nightmare that BLM Gothic depicts. The texts explore Black suffering and death arising from a dehumanizing and insidious necropolitics inherent to the nation.

BLM Gothic extends the observations begun in early Black Gothic texts like Ralph Ellison's *Invisible Man*. As I have detailed elsewhere,[37] *Invisible Man* recounts the multitude of ways African Americans are reduced to nonbeings as their identity and nuanced actualities are displaced by figments of white anxiety. Ellison's narrator remains unnamed throughout the text because the sociopolitics of racist America ultimately deny him a stable, self-constructed identity. He likewise begins and ends the narrative underground in a tomb of sorts located beneath New York City, the centre of American industry and culture in popular constructions. The nation, Ellison argues, is built upon and prospers from Black social and literal death. Richard Wright posits a similar vision of American racial biopolitics in 'The Man Who Lived Underground' as does Amiri Baraka's play *Dutchman*, to name a few examples.

Part of the horror of BLM Gothic stems from the fact that this state of deprivation and erasure persists into the twenty-first century, long after the supposed victories of the US Civil Rights movement, thereby enabling white biopolitical existence. According to Michel Foucault, biopolitics is an inherent aspect of sovereignty which express itself in 'the power and capacity to dictate who is able to live and who must die'.[38] Biopolitics fosters some life and (passively) disallows other life to the point of death. In this dynamic, those subject to death are deemed 'superfluous' and the 'price' of their life 'so meagre that it has no equivalence'.[39] The 'superfluous' life is a drain upon the social economy. Consequently the suffering and death of such populations 'is something to which nobody feels any obligation to respond. Nobody even bears the slightest feelings of responsibility or justice toward this sort of life or, rather, death'.[40]

Though Foucault declares that all political/politicized subjects are caught within this web, Achille Mbembe questions 'But under what practical conditions is the power to kill, to let live, or to expose to death exercised? Who is the subject of this right?'[41] Mbembe codifies this death-dealing aspect of biopolitics as a necropolitical principle that 'stands for organized destruction, for a sacrificial economy, the functioning of which requires, on the one hand, a generalized cheapening of the price of life and, on the other, a habituation to loss'.[42] Equally important, Mbembe insists that racism is its primary driver. While biopolitics produces a 'scission of humanity into "useful" and "useless" – "excess" and

---

[36] Mbembe, *Necropolitics*, p. 17.
[37] See Wester, *African American Gothic*.
[38] Mbembe, *Necropolitics*, p. 46.
[39] Mbembe, *Necropolitics*, pp. 37–38.
[40] Mbembe, *Necropolitics*, p. 38.
[41] Mbembe, *Necropolitics*, p. 38.
[42] Mbembe, *Necropolitics*, p. 40.

"superfluidity"'[43] which can be seen, for example, in the production of the penal colony, Foucault also notes that 'racism is above all a technology aimed at permitting the exercise of biopower'; its specific function 'is to regulate the distribution of death and to make possible the state's murderous functions. It is, he [Foucault] says, "the condition for the acceptability of putting to death"'.[44]

In racially determined biopolitical nations, racial minorities exist in a state of perpetual abjection:

> if, from time to time, they get the nod to move on our level, and are even allowed to associate with us, it is precisely only so that they can be 'thrown back into the dust' – that natural state of debased races. For the slave is not a subject of right but instead a commodity like any other. The most dramatic scene of this throwing back into the dust is lynching.[45]

Black people are made to carry the burden of ancestry and retain the mark of commodity object. In the moment in which the commodity fails to serve and reject exploitation, s/he becomes detritus. As the descendants of enslaved people who were made to labour in the production of US economy, modern Black resistance to remain in such debased states – the determination to exist as citizens – mark them not as human but as the useless excess which must be managed through exposure to deadly risks and dangers. Consequently, biopolitics and its necropolitical ends are a recurrent thematic in BLM Gothic as the practices are productive of actual nightmares.

Biopolitical reduction of Black people to surplus objects appears in numerous BLM Gothic texts. For example, recalling the origin of the 1992 Los Angeles riots, 'The Haint in the Window' notes that 'a Black man's plight was worth less than a dog's (since his neighbor had gotten jail time for beating his dog, unlike those cops who beat Rodney King for the world to see)'.[46] The entire plot of *Get Out* centres around the horrific, very literal reduction of Chris, a talented Black photographer, to the position of a consumable object to be auctioned off amongst elite white consumers (see Figures 1 and 2). Significantly, the film observes how Black intellect and emotion are, at best, merely exploitable aspects of Blackness and, ultimately, excess elements to be thrown into the trash. *Lovecraft Country* likewise marks white reduction of Black people to consumable excess in its plot. Though Christina Braithwhite, who wields the magic taught by the Order of the Ancient Dawn, notes that Atticus is her only remaining family member, she nonetheless plots to bathe in Atticus's blood in order to attain immortality. Of course, Christina's father and the Sons of Adam initially intended to sacrifice Atticus in order to attain immortality as well. The series later reveals that Atticus's entire bloodline was engineered for this purpose as Titus Braithwhite raped his

---

[43] Mbembe, *Necropolitics*, p. 12. [44] Mbembe, *Necropolitics*, p. 71.
[45] Mbembe, *Necropolitics*, p. 18. [46] Due, 'The Haint', p. 37.

Figure 1 Dean Armitage accepts bids for Chris's body

Figure 2 Elite whites friends of the family bid on Chris

slave – Atticus's ancestor – in order to sacrifice the resultant infant as part of a similar ritual. The series argues that the whole of Black existence in America has been a commodity offered up for white consumption.

The figure of Captain Seamus Lancaster, a police captain and an Order of the Ancient Dawn leader, provides an important critique of this practice. Like *Get Out*'s white elites who purchase Blacks in order to claim their bodies so that they – as the new owners/occupants – can experience a different lifestyle, Lancaster extends his life by stealing body parts from Black victims and welding them to his body. The original owners of the parts remain absent, unseen and unheard, throughout the series; they exist only in their contribution to Lancaster's body and are therefore effectively erased. Importantly, Lancaster becomes monstrous in this melding of different body parts, turning himself into a Frankensteinian creature to prolong his life. The series thereby marks the dehumanization and consumption of Black bodies, both literally and figuratively, as horrendous. That this is a recurrent practice of oppressive white bio/necropolitics is apparent in the third episode 'Holy Ghost' in which the ghost of a white scientist who experimented on Black community members – welding pieces of their bodies to other Black bodies – awakens to torment Leti. The episode precedes the revelation of Lancaster's form; the violent haunting spirit, as such, metaphorizes the ways Black communities and populations remain haunted by an oppressive system that reduces them to surplus commodities.

The Ballad of Black Tom similarly performs the necropolitical erasure of Black subjects. The title of the text itself points to the dominance of the displacing fiction and the utter loss of Black subjectivity. The text is split into two halves. The first half follows Charles Thomas Tester, called Charles by his family and Tommy by his friends. The text's performance of loving nicknames recalls the various roles that we play in our different circles, but they always acknowledge the unique individual. We might even consider the sweet, humanizing ring of the nickname 'Tommy' as a signifier of innocent adolescence. The novella in fact portrays Tommy as both witty and naïve in his first adventure as he outwits a dangerous figure while seeming to fulfil her demands. Yet after white police attack Tommy's home and kill Otis, his invalid father, Tommy essentially disappears from the narrative, ending the first half of the novella. In part two, Black Tom displaces Tommy. LaValle renders Black Tom a silent spectre for most of the second half; he exists as a rumour lurking in the shadows, reported on by white witnesses. As one officer explains 'Black Tom is what they all call him . . . . Everywhere he goes, he carries this bloodstained guitar'.[47] Tommy loses his innocence to become a mythic monster evading (white) justice. Racist systemic violence effectively renders Tommy invisible – we might even argue that it kills him alongside his father – and replaces him with a shadowy figure of white anxiety. As one woman explains, she called the police when she saw 'a negro' across the street because 'I was concerned . . . we have two children. I want them to be safe'.[48]

LaValle makes it clear that Tommy's erasure occurs as a result of white systemic racism; Tommy is erased from the narrative in the police interview following Otis's death. In the exchange, only the officers retain individuality even as Tommy speaks:

> The Negro spoke with open disdain and returned Malone's stare so directly that it was Malone who looked away.
> "Your father," Malone said. "Have you buried him yet?"
> "They wouldn't release the body," the Negro said.[49]

As the white officers recount the shooting to Tommy, the novel shifts from referring to Tommy by name to assume the officers' voice: Tommy becomes 'the Negro', his father becomes 'the old Negro', and the community in Red Hook becomes 'the crowd of Negroes'. Importantly, both we and Officer Malone know Tommy's name; reducing him to 'the Negro' therefore signals the erasure of Tommy's humanity and individuality, as does his new nickname Black Tom, a moniker which emphasizes his race as his primary point of definition and identification.

That this erasure serves racist biopolitics and, ultimately, necropolitics is apparent when we consider how the shift recalls Frantz Fanon's encounter and

---

[47] LaValle, *Ballad*, p. 102.   [48] LaValle, *Ballad*, p. 111.   [49] LaValle, *Ballad*, p. 104.

similar erasure as recounted in *Black Skin White Masks*. In the encounter, a white child sees Fanon walking along the street and cries 'Mama, see the Negro! I'm frightened!'[50] Fanon notes how the encounter dehumanizes him, 'batter[ing]' him down to 'tom-toms, cannibalism, intellectual deficiency, fetishism, racial defects, slave-ships', to an animal, a mad 'nigger' – ultimately to a phobogenic object.[51] The cry proves imprisoning; Fanon finds himself caught in a circle drawing ever tighter until the complex individual that is Frantz Fanon disappears beneath the imagined figure that is the phobogenic object called 'negro/nigger'.[52] Significant in Fanon's overview of his erasure is the list of features that displaces his actuality; they all reduce the Black person to a nonentity, and even worse, a threat to be contained if not eradicated. Like Tommy who becomes 'the negro' and finally 'Black Tom', Fanon the handsome intellectual suffocates under the mask of a Gothic nightmare.

BLM Gothic makes reduction to invisibility and monstrosity a supreme point of pain by insisting that there is no minimum age limit to this erasure. Nuotama Bodomo's 'Everybody Dies!' presents newly deceased Black children as the contestants on a game show, their deaths serving as entertainment punctuated by a laugh track. Notably, when a pair of white children wander onto the stage, Rippa the Reaper ushers them out, telling them they are in the wrong place; the place they want has cookies and milk. In *Ghost Boys*, the ghost of twelve-year-old Jerome Rogers discovers after his death that not all neighbourhoods are marred by fences and concrete where grass should be:

> Her school has trees and a track, basketball gym, and football field. My school has a chain-link fence and concrete where I ran and played hoops. Her school is mainly white. Mine was mainly black and Hispanic. Her school has a library with computers. Mine doesn't even have a librarian.
> Being dead, I see places I never saw before. See homes not high-rise projects, schools better than I ever imagined. Who knew there were schools with computer and science labs?[53]

Similar to the milk and cookies awaiting the white children in 'Everybody Dies!' the resources allocated to white schools reveal the extent to which Jerome and his peers are throwaways within the dominant economy of the nation. White children, in contrast, are seen as just that – children who are to be protected, well-educated, nurtured, and comforted. Failure to see Black youths as children and not savages means that the state does not need to invest in them. Thus the segment 'Lethal Letters' in *Everybody Dies!* features fan-mail from

---

[50] Fanon, *Black Skin*, p. 84. [51] Fanon, *Black Skin*, pp. 84, 85. [52] Fanon, *Black Skin*, p. 84.
[53] Rhodes, *Ghost Boys*, p. 113. Jerome's story replicates Tamir Rice's murder; Rice was twelve-years old and shot for playing with a toy gun.

a Black child who explains 'I turned 14 last week, but I've been an adult since the sentencing. There's no kids in prison. There's no hope'. The child's plea to Rippa not to let him turn fifteen renders the 'fan mail' a suicide note. Recasting the tragic imprisonment and consequent suicide of fifteen-year-old Jaquin Thomas[54] even as it recalls the horrific execution of George Stinney,[55] the film short reveals the utterness of Black children's entrapment – the only way to see another way of living is in their death. The horror of the texts stems from the ways Black innocence, humanity, and vulnerability are exiled to invisibility. As the third excerpt for this section observes, Jerome – and the soon-to-be ghost that is Rippa's unnamed fan – is a ghost because authorities failed to see him as a child.

BLM Gothic reminds us that such erasure and displacement occur on a mass scale; though Fanon and Tommy perform it on an individual level, they are single victims in a larger interracial assault. *The Ballad of Black Tom* pauses to describe the lives of Tommy's parents, recounting how hard they worked to attain a level of respectability and stability, even as their labour results in his mother's death at the age of thirty-seven. Though his father lives longer, police shoot him inside his own home with such force that Otis was 'propelled off his mattress and into a wall',[56] Tommy's parents, who are both reduced to 'negroes' in police accounts, illustrate the stakes of the erasure.

Harlem, a predominantly Black space which the novella emphatically humanizes, likewise suffers reduction to disposable phobogenic object. The novel introduces Harlem through the metaphor of a flourishing body, thereby illustrating that the dehumanization of Black Americans occurs simultaneously across a range, from the individual level to the regional level and, implicitly, to the whole of the Black population. Tommy explains that 'Walking through Harlem first thing in the morning was like being a single drop of blood inside an enormous body that was waking up. ... this city lived; day and night it thrived'.[57] Of course, given that the neighbourhood is home to Black Americans and West Indian immigrants, Harlem's body is a Black one. Its body also offers shelter, community, and nurture:

> HARLEM. ONLY AWAY FOR A NIGHT, but he'd missed the company. The bodies close to his on the street, boys running through traffic before the streetlights turned, on their way to school and daring each other to be bold. As he descended the stairs from the station, he smiled.[58]

---

[54] The child was held for weeks without bond in an adult penitentiary where he was attacked by other inmates.

[55] Aged 14 and wrongfully charged with murder, Stinney is the youngest person to be executed in the twentieth-century United States.

[56] LaValle, *Ballad*, pp. 24, 82.   [57] LaValle, *Ballad*, p. 12.   [58] LaValle, *Ballad*, p. 59.

A Black entity, white officers and private citizens reduce the body of Harlem to a beast and render the location a contained wilderness, thereby erasing the nurturing safety offered to its occupants by exposing them to psychosocial violence. In conversing about the area, private detective Howard observes, for instance, 'these people really don't have the same connections to each other as we do. That's been scientifically proven. They're like ants or bees . . . . That's why they can live like this'.[59] The comment alludes to the sense of absolute difference between white and Black subjects, as 'these people' are defined from without as not just lesser, but less even than animals – they are mere bugs. Thus the entire police force arrives heavily armed to ravage Harlem and squash the Harlemites later in the novella.

Candyman (2021) explicitly marks the ways oppressive whiteness defines Black people and communities as commodities exploited for capitalist ends. Anthony's comments on the gentrification of impoverished Black ghettos, quoted among this section's epigraphs, clarify the capitalist gains of biopolitics, noting how urban Black poor populations are passively damned to death in order to render property cheap in an ever-hungry marketplace. Like the horrifying game show stage in 'Everybody Dies!', the Black populace of Cabrini Green are pawns moved about in a board game that they can never influence, much less win. Capitalist culture compounds the effects and mechanisms of biopolitics so that any real and lasting aid to the 'debased race(s)' proves injurious to the dominant society as it thwarts capitalist demands.

In reproducing the systemic, emotional, and physical assaults Black people suffer, BLM Gothic depicts the ways Black subjects are actively and perpetually denied not just humanity but ultimately futurity. Deemed 'backwards' Black subjects are exiled to death zones as sacrifices to white perpetuity. This is the urban ghetto Anthony speaks of which, having served its purpose, is eradicated along with its inhabitants. It is Tommy's Harlem which literally falls to white assault. It is the entirety of the setting for the doomed children in 'Everybody Dies!' Rippa the Reaper, a Black woman who grows weary of the brutal game, is likewise exiled to and entrapped within this death zone. Mourning the young lives that she is forced to batter, shuffle, push and pull across her stage, Rippa throws down her staff and tries to escape through one of the doors only to return to the stage through the other door. The scene truncates the Gothic's traditional escape-capture cycle, thereby marking the brevity of the seeming reprieves from violence and the progress Blacks seem to make towards racial equality.

The very fates of the protagonists insist upon the Gothic existence and perpetual entrapment of Black Americans. As Suydam explains to his Black

---

[59] LaValle, *Ballad*, pp. 61–62.

guests in his ploy to garner their support, the disenfranchisement and violence non-whites suffer are demanded by and performed for an unseen power[60] that we might call 'white hegemony'. Atticus's entire bloodline was engineered to be a sacrifice to white immortality. *Candyman*'s Anthony was fated to become another Candyman, in the midst of a multitude of Candymen, despite his temporary escape to another area. And nothing Black – not even the Reaper – can escape death zones while the disembodied white MC continues to govern the narrative. The origin point of BLM Gothic's terror is the recognition that Black people remain targeted by such necroeconomy.

BLM Gothic clearly defines US necropolitical mechanisms while marking each of these mechanisms as points of horror by aligning them with Gothic tropes. The first instance of this is in the depiction of the Gothic ruinous and haunted location. In BLM Gothic, this is the segregated Black and Brown region, usually an impoverished inner-city location, that is, the ghetto.[61] The ghetto proves a sign of necropolitics because they are spaces in which the entire population is a target as their 'Daily life is militarized. .... Local civil institutions are systematically destroyed. .... Invisible killing is added to outright executions'.[62] The Black neighbourhood is the place of utter containment similar to what Fanon notes in his description of colonial subjugation:

> The town belonging to the colonized people, or at least the native town, the Negro village ... is a place of ill fame, peopled by men of evil repute. They are born there, it matters little where or how; they die there, it matters not where, nor how. It is a world without spaciousness; men live there on top of each other, and their huts are built one on top of the other. The native town is a hungry town, starved of bread, of meat, of shoes, of coal, of light. The native town is a crouching village, a town on its knees, a town wallowing in the mire. It is a town of niggers and dirty Arabs.[63]

As Fanon's comments observe, the Black and Brown space is the phobogenic locale, one filled with less-than-people, citizens reduced down to oppressive stereotypes like 'niggers' and 'Arabs'. The ghetto is not just a dumping ground for the impoverished but a prison for the unruly 'savages' outcasted from 'civilized' society. A location of active disinvestment and neglect, populated by the socially dead, the US ghetto is a Gothic region, haunted by the undead, the monstrous, and the soon-to-be dead.

---

[60] LaValle, *Ballad*, p. 49.
[61] Although recent years have seen a resistance to using the term 'ghetto', I use the term here because of its historical resonance with the neighborhoods Nazis forced Jews to live in before ultimately removing them to the death camps. The modern American iteration collapses the two locations, rendering the Black ghetto the place of oppression and death.
[62] Mbembe, *Necropolitics*, pp. 82–83. [63] Fanon, *Wretched*, p. 39.

The Black ghetto became a recurrent trope in Horror films and, more importantly, in American culture in the 1980s. Films across various genres depicted ghettos as primarily Black spaces populated by violent and future criminals.[64] As Robin Means Coleman explains, 'the dominant message ... was that cities were savage, lawless terrains to which the most irredeemable in our society – the underclass and people of color, two groups often understood to be one and the same – should be consigned. ... these were images of decaying or "dead" cities, reflecting a post-White flight America'.[65] These spaces were unsafe for all but were especially dangerous for white people. As such, popular white Horror reiterated the anxiety of the colonizer/oppressor: 'the look that the native turns on the settler's town is a look of lust, a look of envy; it expresses his dreams of possession–all manner of possession'.[66]

BLM Gothic maintains the mythos of the ghetto as a death zone but with an important difference – the fictions insistently depict ghettos as white-created spaces and methods for segregating and confining Blacks. As Anthony notes, 'the hood' is a manufactured area which deals out death passively. In 'Haint in the Window' Darryl, reflecting on the new nickname for the gentrified neighbourhood – *The Garden* – 'almost laugh[s]' given its former state as an 'eyesore he'd walked past his whole life'.[67] Similar to Anthony, he recalls how 'Residents had been begging for a new paint job for twenty years, but new paint only came with the reopening. The evictions'.[68] Like Fanon's Black/native towns, deprivation characterizes US urban ghettos. Urban ghettos are places with few grocers and little fresh fruit and vegetables; instead, fast food chains, and liquor stores dominate the areas. They are places without banks; instead, a preponderance of check-cashing businesses operates in the neighbourhoods. So utter is their containment that the neighbourhoods rarely have Post Offices; the 'nigger' is denied even the possibility of reaching out beyond their region by mail.[69]

These 'death zones' are modern iterations of the unruly colony – the original site of necropolitical violence. Like the rebellious colonies, the ghetto is supposedly populated by 'savages' whose 'armies do not form a distinct

---

[64] Slang for Black ghettos like 'the jungle' and 'the street' refer both to the wildness of such locations and the impossibility of domesticating the space and its population as the residents all live on 'the street'. Even the seemingly harmless pejorative 'the hood' marks the space as an unfinished and inhospitable location, missing as it is the 'neighbor(ly)' part of 'neighborhood'.
[65] Means Coleman, *Horror Noire*, p. 145. [66] Fanon, *Wretched*, p. 39.
[67] Due, 'The Haint', p. 33. [68] Due, 'The Haint', p. 33.
[69] There is a vast amount of research on and depictions of such government disinvestment. See fiction such as Lorraine Hansberry's *A Raisin in the Sun* (1959) and Richard Wright's *Native Son* (1940) as well as studies like Loïc Wacquant's *Urban Outcasts* (2008) Brandi Blesset's 'Urban Renewal and "Ghetto" Development in Baltimore' (2020) and Henry Louis Taylor Jr.'s 'Disrupting Market-based Predatory Development' (2020).

entity'.[70] It is impossible for the state to negotiate peace in these areas; rather 'the violence of the state of exception is deemed to operate in the service of "civilization"'.[71] The ghetto is the created wasteland peopled by supposedly dangerous Others who must be controlled through neglect at best and brutality at worse. Black people are deemed so 'savage' and 'different' from white Americans – the site of normality, citizenship and, ultimately, humanity – that Black life

> is just another form of animal life, a horrifying experience, something alien beyond imagination or comprehension. .. ... Savages are, as it were, 'natural' human beings who lack a specifically human character, a specifically human reality, 'so that when European men massacred them they somehow were not aware that they had committed murder'.[72]

The police attack on Harlem which concludes *The Ballad of Black Tom* exemplifies this erasure and reduction to disposable savagery. Sanctioned, regularized terror proves a common feature of such locations. Black ghettos – populated with people like Chris and Atticus who exist at best as objects for consumption, or at worst populated by people like Tom and Anthony who actively resist white domination – are locations in which violence is necessitated and any impulse towards empathy with the residents/victims is nullified.

William Burke's story of the rise of another Candyman best exemplifies BLM Gothic's depiction of Black communities as necropolitical 'death zones'. In answer to Anthony's question 'what's Candyman', Burke tells the story of his encounter with and the murder of Sherman Fields. As Burke's narrative begins, the film flashes back to Cabrini Green in the 1970s. Panned out at a distance from Sherman, Cabrini Green is a series of rundown apartment blocks surrounded by concrete and dead trees (see Figure 3). Sherman's introduction also marks the entire neighbourhood as a site figured as monstrous through the visual association with Sherman alongside the complete erasure of signs of life and vitality. The trees are skeletal in this vision of Cabrini Green, and the lacklustre brown housing suggests a prison rather than homes.

As Burke's narrative continues, the camera pans over to reveal two police officers sitting in their cars at the edge of the location, surveilling the neighbourhood for a suspected criminal (see Figure 4). At the sound of young Burke's scream, the officers in the car rush into one of the buildings, followed by a great number of other police. The brevity between Burke's scream and the arrival of the mass of officers reveal that there were far more than two officers watching the

---

[70] Mbembe, *Necropolitics*, p. 77. Stereotypes of gang violence in urban ghettos constitute such armies, as each gang defends its area and engages in combat with other gangs and general interlopers into the area.
[71] Mbembe, *Necropolitics*, p. 77.   [72] Mbembe, *Necropolitics*, pp. 77–78.

Figure 3 Sherman Fields in front of Cabrini Green

Figure 4 Police cars outside of Cabrini Green tenement

location the entire time. Burke's narration explains that the officers suspected someone in Cabrini Green was responsible for putting razors into children's Halloween candy in a white neighbourhood. The officers beat Sherman to death; yet a couple weeks later, more razor blades appear in the candy of white children. What the film does not say but makes implicit is the illogic of suspecting that anyone in the ghetto would be responsible for the crime. The white victims would have lived in neighbourhoods inaccessible to the impoverished Black populace. The police surveillance and excessive number of officers who arrive to 'detain' Sherman point to a predetermined idea of the ghetto and its populace as savage monsters.

The construction of Black people renders their murders acceptable, if not sanctioned, by the larger population. As previously discussed, the erasure of Black individuality, humanity, and subjectivity is an important feature of necropolitics, and when we consider the wide-scale sanctioning and production of death, we can understand why. There is no protest over Sherman's death because he was not a man but a monster; yet officers roughly push past young Burke on the stairs instead of pausing to offer aid because he too is subhuman. By defining the 'ghetto' as a space of horror, the entire community – including its youngest members – disappear under the visage of monstrosity. Thus no one mourns their suffering and deaths, be it by a slow passive murder through deprivation or a brutal and violent assault. Jerome speaks to this when he mourns 'My neighborhood's poor, segregated. . . . . .. Didn't know how much I was living in a danger zone. But why did cops fear me?'[73] Although Jerome's narrative begins with an account of the daily threats he faces in

---

[73] Rhodes, *Ghost Boys*, p. 149.

his community, it is not the bullies or even the drug dealers that render his neighbourhood a danger zone. Rather, it is the fear the cops hold of him, his community and his family that render his area truly dangerous.

Distressingly Blacks learn to see each other through this necropolitical lens and to read each other as the rumoured monsters. When young Burke first sees Sherman, a man who has long lived in the area, emerging from a hole in the wall, his reaction is not one of sympathy and concern but one of terror. Similarly, Tommy fails to actually see the Black and Brown West Indians of his neighbourhood and believes places like the Victorian society are dangerous and seedy businesses. Tommy, however, at least has the chance to recognize the truth of such places – they are quite mundane and nurturing:

> The shorthand for a den of crime and sin? The place where Harlem's worst criminals were too afraid to go? He'd assumed he knew what kind of place this would be.
> .... why wouldn't the Victoria Society be like those legendary opium dens? Or had Tommy simply assumed terrible things about this wave of West Indian immigrants? .... And now he'd come to find the Victoria Society might as well be a British tearoom. .... Being inside now, seeing this place truly, was like learning another world existed within – or alongside – the world he'd always known. Worse, all this time he'd been too ignorant to realize it.[74]

In addition to breaking the myth of the hyper-Black, impoverished area as a place of lawlessness and terror, Tommy's commentary also reminds us that the depiction of the Black population is a fiction in the service of white necroeconomy. More importantly, it is a fiction taught to white and Black populations, even those residing in the zones marked for death.

Unsurprisingly, such locations do not sustain, much less foster, life; rather life continues there in spite of state disinvestment. This disinvestment is yet another source of shudders in BLM Gothic: the large-scale production of death through various means. In addition to the lack of resources and consumer services characterizing the locations is a profound lack of life-saving services. State disinvestment in such locations is essentially an orchestrated siege and 'systemic sabotage of ... societal and urban infrastructure network .... in other words, infrastructural warfare'.[75] Such warfare occurs alongside 'the appropriation of land, water, and airspace resources'[76] thereby revealing that warfare is a product of capitalist desire, rather than necessitated by the 'savagery' of a populace. Anthony's critique of the creation of 'the hood' defines this dynamic clearly. Infrastructural warfare acts as an invisible force which residents can

---

[74] LaValle, *Ballad*, pp. 29–30. [75] Mbembe, *Necropolitics*, p. 82.
[76] Mbembe, *Necropolitics*, p. 82.

neither see nor fight but which they certainly suffer from as they die from supposedly self-inflicted injuries which, in reality, can be traced back to a lack of resources and systemic support. Thus Darryl recalls a long list of residents who met untimely but 'natural' deaths:

> how many other customers had died since Darryl started working here when he was fifteen, their hair graying, walking slowly, persistent coughs shaking stooping shoulders, breaths wheezing under the weight of cigarettes, heart conditions, and diabetes? Three dozen, easily. And those were just the ones whose names he remembered, whose faces had graced the aisles with laughter and smiles.[77]

Similarly as Jerome's ghost explores Chicago beyond his impoverished neighbourhood, he discovers 'Chicago is more beautiful than I ever thought. I didn't know there were parks with swings, slides, running and bicycle tracks. I didn't know there were over a hundred skyscrapers. Or Lincoln Park Zoo, with African penguins striped black and white'.[78] The comment alludes to the utterness of Black confinement and state disinvestment as Jerome is amazed to discover Chicago's well-known skyline alongside a number of other basic amenities. As such BLM Gothic continues the tradition begun by Black Horror films of the 1990s which 'reveal[ed] that what was most threatening to urban Blacks, the stuff that haunted them while awake and in their dreams, was lingering racism, socioeconomic disparities, health crises, and specific forms of criminality'.[79] In BLM Gothic, the urban ghetto is a space of horror because it exists, not because of who is forced to exist in it.[80]

Sanctioned anti-Black violence committed by private citizens haunts much of BLM Gothic. Two of the most impactful and difficult episodes of *Lovecraft Country*, 'Jig-a-Bobo' (episode 8) and 'Rewind 1921' (episode 9) reproduce scenes of private anti-Black violence from history. The bulk of 'Rewind 1921' takes place in Tulsa just before and during the white massacre that destroyed the

---

[77] Due, 'The Haint', p. 42. Haunting this list is the question of access to medical treatment and emergency services. As Public Enemy famously protested in the song '911 is a Joke', 'If your life is on the line then you're dead today/Latecomers with the late coming stretcher/That's a body bag in disguise y'all, I'll betcha/I call 'em body snatchers cause they come to fetch ya/with an autopsy ambulance just to dissect ya'. Public Enemy, '911 is a Joke', *Fear of a Black Planet*, Kobalt Music, 1990, CD. Such abuse can be traced back to slavery and medical experimentation on unanesthetized slaves; one of the horror stories arising from antebellum America is the folktale of the Night Doctors, also known as the Ku Klux doctors.

[78] Rhodes, *Ghost Boys*, p. 134.   [79] Means Coleman, *Horror Noire*, p. 175.

[80] Of course, most Black Americans do not live in ghettos, as films like *Get Out* (2017) and series such as *Them* (2021) remind us. *Lovecraft Country* does not take place in a ghetto but in an all-Black segregated part of Chicago which suffers from similar systemic necropolitics. The ghetto proves a way to metaphorize the systemic containment which Black Americans suffer regardless of their actual locations and socioeconomic status.

Black community there. Similar to Tommy's depiction of Harlem as a haven, the episode spends a significant portion of time following the everyday activities of the Black Tulsa residents on a brightly lit day. As night descends, the community becomes a place of horror as armed white men appear attacking random Black residents, setting fire to houses, shooting some residents and beating others to death. The episode concludes with a reminder of Black humanity and lost life as Montrose watches Tulsa burn, narrating what cannot be shown:

> Peg Leg Taylor's last stand on Standpipe Hill. Oh, that was something. Still, they burned down Byar's Tailor Shop. Dr. Jackson, 'best Negro surgeon in all America' ... Shot in the face. Mrs. Rodgers lost her invalid daughter. White Phelps took in Negroes, hid 'em in the basement. Commodore Knox. They did him in the worst. And Thomas?[81]

Occurring just after the scene in which Atticus's ancestor slowly burns alive, Montrose's monologue marks the destruction of Black life as a point of horror and pain which still haunts, given the monologue ends with a question. Yet in reproducing the destruction of Tulsa, the series marks how such excessive violence was implicitly sanctioned by the state and nation given no one was prosecuted for the murders in the actual event.

The episode 'Jig-a-Bobo' also opens with a moment exemplifying sanctioned anti-Black violence from history: Emmett Till's lynching. Significantly, we do not see Emmett Till's corpse; rather we see the outpouring of pain across the community. The episode stresses the heat of the day and the consequent stench which pervades the Black Chicago neighbourhood during Till's wake. The stench itself implies that the horrible odour of the corpse extends to the whole of the Black community, who are marked as the walking dead. The choice not to show Till's body is as important and impactful as Mamie Till's insistence on displaying it at the actual wake in 1955. As Magnolia Cooksey-Mathious, a friend of Emmett Till, recollects of the wake, 'This was our friend layin' looking like a monster'.[82] Others like Richard Heard noted that the sight of Till's corpse was an encounter with horror: 'it was grotesque .... I couldn't sleep at night. It was traumatic for me for – for months'.[83] The show, however, refuses to reproduce the Black body as monstrous corpse, and instead focuses on the horrifying violence that reduces the Black individual to a horrifying cadaver. The choice parallels the depiction of Dee's flight from Lancaster's curse – the terrifying stereotypes of Blackness, a monstrous Topsy and Bopsy (Figure 5). Their faces warped into horrific smiles,

---

[81] *Lovecraft Country,* 'Rewind 1921', HBO, 11 October 2020, television series.
[82] *The American Experience,* 'The Murder of Emmett Till'.
[83] *The American Experience,* 'The Murder of Emmett Till'.

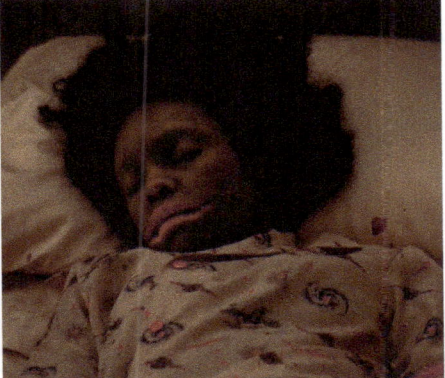

Figure 5 Topsy and Bopsy

Figure 6 Dee, possessed by Topsy and Bopsy

the two spectres are barely human. Their appearance stands in for the monstrosity of Till's corpse. Dee flees from figures signifying warping stereotypes of Blackness as well as physical assaults that warp Black bodies in death (Figure 6). The stereotype of Black savagery is marked as productive of death through the episode's symbology and turn to an actual historical event.

BLM Gothic argues that such violence serves as part of the systemic terror defining Black existence in America; the violence done by private citizens is not only sanctioned by legal and justice systems but works in collusion with them. LaValle stresses this point multiple times over in *Destroyer*. For instance, volume 2 shows a group of anti-immigrant citizens waiting at the US-Mexico border when the Creature breaches the wall, killing the immigrants fleeing behind him. In their conversation, the militiamen reveal the relationship between their technically illegal work and government agencies: 'Border patrol tipped us off, of course. They love the work we're doing'.[84] Akai's death more tragically defines the collusion between unarmed citizens and armed government officials. The panels recounting the day of his death begin with three small panels of Akai playing in a baseball match and waving goodbye to his teammates. The fourth and largest panel is of a wealthy neighbourhood; Akai is small in the background as he walks to a bus stop. In silhouette, a woman looks out of her window, hidden, anonymous and on the phone with police officers, declaring 'there's a man with a rifle walking in front of my house. . . . . He's Black. . . . . 18? Maybe 20'.[85] Akai, a twelve-year-old, carries only a baseball bat, and is well-past the woman's house in the scene. The anonymous woman's call leads

---

[84] LaValle, *Destroyer* vol. 2.   [85] LaValle, *Destroyer* vol. 5.

to Akai's death; if the police officers are a weapon aimed at 'offenders' then the private citizen aims them. LaValle expands on the scene in the concluding comments to the volume:

> In many ways, this is the most important scene in this entire series. No phone call, no story.
> .... Conversations about police brutality tend to be treated like a line – at one end there's the police and at the other the person being brutalized. But sometimes police brutality is a triangle: the police, the person being brutalized, and the person who called the cops.
> .... We can't have honest conversations about brutality against people of color if we don't discuss who called in the brutalizer.[86]

LaValle's observations define a central horror of BLM Gothic – the extent to which even an unarmed citizen can be a death-dealer to Black citizens.

Iterations of anti-Black warfare engaged by private citizens alludes to the even larger concern of BLM Gothic: the extent to which 'the sovereign might kill [Black subjects] at any time or in any manner'.[87] As horrifying as it is to confront such violence from private citizens who are implicitly sanctioned to do so, the nature of the exchange – occurring between private citizens – provides some hope for self-defence, minimal though it may be. However, when agents of the state are the primary sources of terror for Black subjects, even that small bit of hope dies. Thus BLM Gothic texts consistently depict Black communities as over-policed locations. Importantly, the appearance of the police never provides comfort but rather marks the locations as terrorized – rather than terrorizing – places. Police officers seem to be everywhere surveilling Atticus and his friends in *Lovecraft Country*; likewise, they are a common presence in Tommy's Harlem long before they wage an actual war on the residents.

The police assault on Harlem, briefly discussed earlier, best exemplifies the violence and horror of such infrastructural warfare. Already confined to an impoverished area and the subject of over-surveillance, the population suffers an actual assault of such intensity that the neighbourhood becomes a literal warzone:

> the officers had a bevy of weapons as they prepared to take the three tenements. Each man wore his department-issue revolver, but now, from the rear of the emergency trucks, an arsenal appeared. .... Three Browning Model 1921 heavy machine guns were set up on the street. Each required three men to take it down from the trucks. They were set in a row; each one's long barrel faced the front stoop of a tenement. They looked like a trio of cannons, better for a ground war than breaching the front doors of a building.
> When the 1921s were set down, they were so heavy chips of tarmac were thrown in the air. .... These guns were designed to shoot airplanes out of the

---

[86] LaValle, *Destroyer* vol. 5.   [87] Mbembe, *Necropolitics*, p. 78.

sky. Much of the local population had fled countries under siege, in the midst of war, and had not expected to find such artillery used against citizens of the United States.[88]

Positioned as at the peak of the novella, the excessive siege makes the horrifying violence of the infrastructural warfare visible. The infrastructural violence the residents suffer at the hands of the officers and a negligent government is merely a passive form of the artillery aimed at them in the above scene; the forms it takes are as varied and deadly as the assortment of weapons the residents confront in the final assault. The irony of the final line is that the Harlemites are not under siege from their own country because the United States has never accepted them, regardless of their national origin or immigration status. The absurdity of aiming a canon at the door to a tenement building vanishes when one considers how the weapon comments upon the target. Like Sherman, the Harlemites become 'bodies stripped of being ... quickly returned to the state of simple skeletons, simple residues of an unburied pain; emptied and insignificant corporeities'.[89] The scene disturbs because of how the guns reduce the people and community to subhuman yet nightmarish fodder.

These instances of police anti-Black violence are inherently Gothic not just because they actively terrorize masses of Black victims; and not just because they warp communities which were havens from private violence into utter death zones. This kind of violence is Gothic because of how it reproduces history in the current era and, further, of how it guarantees the perpetuation of that history into the future. It also horrifies because the violence knows no spatial bounds. While Tommy's story takes place in early twentieth-century Harlem, its aspects are repeated in Atticus's middle-classed Black community in mid twentieth-century Chicago, in Sherman's impoverished and Anthony's gentrified Cabrini Greens, in the Armitage's elite New York suburb and in Chris's modern Brooklyn,[90] and all across the twenty-first century mid-Atlantic United States in *Destroyer*. Most poignantly, in 'Everybody Dies!' Rippa the Reaper's gameshow board is a map of America, with lights appearing across the entire country. The stage itself is in the netherworld and thus denies a sense of spatial and temporal limitations; rather anti-Black violence occurs anywhere and everywhere at any moment. BLM Gothic shudders in confronting the reality of how '[racial] terror intertwines with [racially] generated fantasies of wilderness, and death and fictions'.[91] Such moments of sadness and horrifying loss are part of the way that BLM Gothic marks the ideology of Black

---

[88] LaValle, *Ballad*, pp. 116–117.   [89] Mbembe, *Necropolitics*, p. 36.
[90] While *Get Out* largely takes place in upstate New York, the film starts in Chris's home in Brooklyn, implying that the Armitage's reach extends beyond their area.
[91] Mbembe, *Necropolitics*, p. 78.

'savagery' and critiques it as a point of horror not because it is true but because of how it allows us to accept profound anti-Black violence as inevitable, if not necessary.

BLM Gothic reveals how Black victims suffer a curse that kills them multiple times over beyond even their actual death. As the subjects of necropolitical assault, they suffer a social death that makes their actual suffering and deaths negligible. Anthony in *Candyman* best exemplifies this issue. As Burke explains, Anthony was destined to become a Candyman from birth, and, like Sherman, remain unmourned and unvindicated in his death. He is also doomed to suffer persecution while very much alive. We must, for example, observe that Sherman was missing a hand before his brutal murder. The film never explains the bodily injury; instead, we are left to presuppose that the injury was a result of previous violence.[92] To add insult to injury, Sherman is forced to retreat into the tenement's walls where he hides from the cops. He essentially becomes a rodent or insect as the undesirable, wall-dwelling pest that is eventually stomped to death. Even after Sherman's innocence becomes apparent, children in the area tell stories that reduce Sherman to a predatory monster. This is Anthony's Gothic fate: a life of assault and grievous bodily injury, sanctioned murder, a denial of mourning and, ultimately, the erasure of his humanity and actual self. Multiple times in the film, when Anthony looks in the mirror, he sees Sherman staring back at him. Yet given the army of Candymen revealed in the film's end credits (Figure 7), Anthony is not exceptional in this curse.

Destroyer and 'Haint in the Window' similarly gesture to this sense of fate. Jo, in recounting her life with Akai from his infancy to his preteen years to the

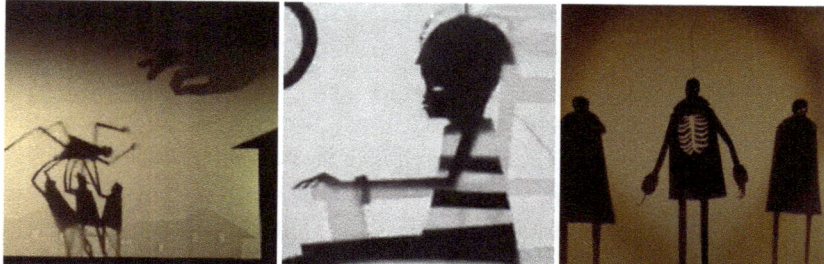

Figure 7 Shadow puppets from *Candyman* (2021) end credits

---

[92] The film subtly references the original Candyman story. Daniel Robitaille is robbed of his hand in the midst of the lynching that turns him into Candyman; the lack of explanation for Sherman's missing hand gestures back to Robitaille's assault while also stretching the violence across the span of Sherman's life.

night of his shooting, remarks 'I had tenure. Akai attended St. Ignatius. I thought we'd made it. I assumed we were safe. But I was wrong'.[93] Importantly, volume 3 opens with the day of Akai's death as Jo worries over letting him travel to his baseball game alone. Together they review Akai's planned route to the game. Jo comments that Akai has planned well, yet she remains afraid of letting him ride the Chicago city train alone. Her insistence on intricately planning his route metaphorizes Jo's life and hopes – her drive to earn an advanced education, to achieve an upper-middle class socioeconomic status, to enrol Akai in a prestigious school are all iterations of meticulous life-mapping for herself and her child in order to ensure safety. Even Akai's chosen sport serves this plan, given that baseball is a decisively American sport, played only in the United States, among its territories, in formerly occupied countries and in places where the United States exercises great imperialistic influence. Akai is the 'all-American' child, yet Jo remains haunted by the precarious nature of Black existence in America. Despite all of her planning, she is wrong in assuming their safety; Akai is doomed to die.

Similarly, Darryl realizes the ghost that has been haunting him is not a figure from the past but the ghost of his future. Furthermore, Daryll is just one of many to suffer unnatural but seemingly inevitable deaths: 'His parents were gone, killed by a drunk driver on Crenshaw when he was thirty. . . . . His Aunt Lucy and Uncle Boo. His cousin Ray. Dead, all of them. They were ghosts haunting him even when they didn't make themselves known'.[94] But only in the moment of his death does he realize that this haunting is not just the spectre of memory but the promise of his fate:

> Darryl noticed a figure reflected in the glass, too far away to be him–and yet, it was him. The same eyes he'd seen from behind the desk now stared up at him up close with an expression that seemed to say: *Do you get it now, brother?*
> . . . . He'd had a feeling about this security guard from the moment he saw him. And he still hadn't read the signs.[95] [italic in the original]

Darryl's recollection of the figure's seeming distance even as it is also him reiterates the notion of his death as a curse and his predestined end. He is both ghost of the past and spectre of the future, seemingly far away but already here.

Characters like Anthony, Darryl, and the many previously mentioned others are the norm, predestined to violent death by virtue of their skin color. Horrifically this is the normative practice of necropolitical societies: 'Habituation to sadism, the implacable will to know nothing, to experience no empathy toward the victims, to be persuaded of the natives' villainy, to hold them responsible for the atrocities as well as the exactions and massive damages inflicted upon them – such was [is] the

---

[93] LaValle, *Destroyer* vol. 3.   [94] Due, 'The Haint', p. 42.   [95] Due, 'The Haint', p. 48.

law'.⁹⁶ Recycled from the incredibly old and violent politics of monarchical sovereignty, these 'habits' make ghosts out of the living while they still breathe. In pointing out this dynamic, BLM Gothic reinserts empathy by insisting we confront and know this warping and destructive sociopolitical state, and reminds us to scream at the sadism. In doing so, the mode reclaims Blacks from the sacrificial borders of society to mark the psychosocial and physical violence done to Blacks as the real point of monstrous horror.

2 Making Whiteness Strange

> The monstrous does not lie solely in its embodiment ... nor its location ... nor in the process(es) through which it enacts its being, but also (indeed, perhaps primarily) in its impact.⁹⁷

> Racism bloats and disfigures the face of the culture that practices it.⁹⁸

> Nobody ever thinks of himself as a villain, does he? Even monsters hold high opinions of themselves.⁹⁹

In the introduction to his study of whiteness, Richard Dyer argues that in order to dismantle systems of white dominance and oppression, whiteness must be dethroned from its claim to speaking (and acting) for humanity. Race, Dyer contends, is something applied only to non-white people who can only speak for their specific race. White people, in contrast, are not racially seen much less named, and thus 'function as a human norm. Other people are raced, we are just people'.¹⁰⁰ Existing outside of race, whiteness claims ownership of the 'human'. This construction – whites as the sole proprietors of humanity – secures dominance and power.¹⁰¹ The only way to dislodge whiteness 'from the position of power, with all the inequities, oppression, privileges and sufferings in its train' and dismantle 'the authority with which they/we speak and act in and on the world' is by racing, or essentially 'seeing', whiteness along with all of its particularities.¹⁰² In other words, we have to make whiteness 'strange'.

Representing whiteness as alienating, horrifying, and 'strange' is an integral element of BLM Gothic in which whiteness is not only the point of violence but also chaos, irrationality, and inhumanity. While BLM Gothic mourns Blacks' understandable turns to a level of rage and violence which might be condemned as monstrous, as the next section will discuss, it repeatedly names whiteness as the origin of monstrosity. The white villains in BLM Gothic span the range from

---

⁹⁶ Mbembe, *Necropolitics*, pp. 127–128.   ⁹⁷ Mittman, 'Introduction', pp. 1–14.
⁹⁸ Text of Frantz Fanon's speech before the First Congress of Negro Writers and Artists in Paris, September 1956. Published in *Presence Africaine*, special issue (June–November, 1956), pp. 31–44 (p. 37).
⁹⁹ LaValle, *Ballad*, p. 48.   ¹⁰⁰ Dyer, *White*, pp. 1–2.   ¹⁰¹ Dyer, *White*, p. 9.
¹⁰² Dyer, *White*, p. 2.

exceptionally powerful figures to absolutely mundane citizens. In presenting 'normative' whiteness as the source of horror, BLM Gothic disconnects the monstrous from superficial differences such that 'The monstrous does not lie solely in its embodiment ... nor its location ... nor in the process(es) through which it enacts its being, but also (indeed, perhaps primarily) in its *impact*',[103] Whites in BLM Gothic texts perform and embody a banal evil, in so much as the violence characters perform is 'accepted, routinized, and implemented without moral revulsion and political indignation and resistance'[104] from those other than its victims. BLM Gothic is therefore in keeping with contemporary shifts in Horror in which the monster is not the marginalized other but normative-seeming psychopaths (like *American Psycho*'s Patrick Bateman), corrupt corporate entities (for instance, *Resident Evil*'s Umbrella Corp), and conspiring governments (such as in *The Cabin in the Woods*). However, while scholars like Jeffrey Weinstock[105] note that this new figure of monstrosity betrays a distrust in hegemonic structures, the monsters of white-centred Horror plots, while not marginal, are nonetheless exceptions to otherwise decent and humane cultures and populations. Norman Bates and Patrick Bateman are outliers in their group; their psychopathology is a sign of an internal disorder particular to them. The entirety of the corporation and government is not corrupt, but rather a particular cabal within the larger entity proves the source of villainy. The assumption of modern Horror remains that there is a pure, underlying base culture and society which has been defiled; any abhuman whiteness is a genetic mutation, not the shared sign of the (white) human.

BLM Gothic rejects the assumption that there is an underlying purity to American sociopolitics. Rejecting the Eurocentric vision of humanity which depends upon anti-Blackness 'to define its own limits and to designate humanity as an achievement as well as to give form to the category of "the animal"',[106] BLM Gothic designates (white) humanity an achievement in brutality which gives form to the category only of the brutalized and the other. If sixteenth-century Europeans deemed Africa 'a land of new monsters',[107] then twenty-first century America is a land of old ones, and the white human(ity) is characteristically abhuman. The mode's depictions stress that America was founded and dependent upon racial subjugation, land theft, and outright genocidal assault. As Achille Mbembe explains, it is not a coincidence that democracy in the West unfolded alongside colonial expansion and the pro-slavery state.[108] Modern

---

[103] Mittman, 'Introduction', p. 7.   [104] Arendt, *Eichmann in Jerusalem*, p. 287.
[105] Weinstock list four specific categories of invisible monstrosity as it appears in Horror films since the late twentieth century. For more, see Weinstock, 'Invisible Monsters'.
[106] Jackson, *Becoming Human*, p. 4.   [107] Jackson, *Becoming Human*, p. 6.
[108] Mbembe, *Necropolitics*, p. 22.

democracy grew alongside the rise of the capitalist market which is inherently 'a bloody process of devouring (when it comes to destroying, without return, the life of beings and species)'.[109] The US sociopolitical system was monstrous from its birth, evincing in its origin 'tolerance for a certain political violence, including illegal forms of it' and has 'integrated forms of brutality into their [its] culture, forms borne by a range of private institutions acting on top of the state, whether irregular forces, militias, or other paramilitary or corporatist formations'.[110] Consequently, in recent years, Black Gothic has stressed an amorphous antagonist as the ultimate monster which is embodied in and abetted by white Americans. For example, 'Everybody Dies!' features a white-sounding voice as the game show narrator; this narrator persists in pushing the show forward despite Rippa's despair and attempted escapes. Similarly, while *Destroyer* features two white villains – Frankenstein's original creature and the megalomaniacal Director – both are nonetheless minions created and directed by an even larger, unseen force.

Central to the maniacal power of white hegemony in BLM Gothic is dominance over narrative.[111] As much as each iteration of Candyman is a creation of a particular moment of sanctioned anti-Black violence, Candyman's concluding comment – '*They* will say you were innocent'[112] [italic added for emphasis] – alludes to an unknown quantity and populace. The faceless 'they' has the power to decide who is the praiseworthy victim and who is the chaotic monster, thereby ultimately determining Black fate through narrative. Such narratological manipulations and dissemination proves another 'technology of racist power'[113] as it reiterates tales of Black villainy to Americans, including Blacks themselves, rendering Blacks victims twice over – firstly, as noted in Section 1, by predefining them as monstrous and secondly, by re-articulating any Black resistance as a point of horror, thereby nullifying Blacks' attempts at revolution before they begin. These narrative manipulations, working alongside 'the ritual of execution', act to 'sow terror in the minds of its victims and revive the lethal passions underpinning white supremacy'.[114] In continuing to point to a greater hegemonic structure that exercises very personal violence through actual weapons and weaponizing narratives, the texts render the whole of the US landscape a point of terror.

---

[109] Mbembe, *Necropolitics*, p. 14. [110] Mbembe, *Necropolitics*, pp. 16–17.
[111] In this way, BLM Gothic grapples with the 'Fake News'/post-fact/post-truth era. A number of scholars have explored how the era of disinformation particularly targets racial, ethnic, and religious minority groups. See, for example, Kimberly Grambo, 'Fake News and Racial, Ethnic, and Religious Minorities: A Precarious Quest for Truth' (2019); Charlotte Galpin and Patrick Vernon, 'Post-truth politics as discursive violence: Online abuse, the public sphere and the figure of "the expert"' (2023); Rachel Kuo and Alice Marwick, 'Critical disinformation studies: History, power, and politics' (2021).
[112] *Candyman* (2021), emphasis added. [113] Mbembe, *Necropolitics*, p. 18.
[114] Mbembe, *Necropolitics*, p. 18.

Nor does such horror stop at the framework of the country; rather these sociopolitics cultivate a (white) population and political industry that not only accepts violent suppression and dehumanization but which happily engages in it. As noted in the previous section, necropolitics depends upon the reduction of targeted groups from the place of the human to the place of the phobogenic object. The threat and horror attached to such 'objects' do not arise out of a void but rather are in part reflections of white fear about (justified) Black revolt and (rational) vengeance.[115] As a consequence, 'confronted with a Negro one is unable to behave oneself and act "normally"'.[116] In other words, the sociopolitical origins of the US coupled with its persistently violent history produces a neurotic population given to violence. Therefore in BLM Gothic, the horror is not that any (white) citizen might be a psychopath but rather that they are likely all psychopaths who have mastered 'indifference to objective signs of cruelty'.[117] BLM Gothic wonders who among the white American population is safe/sane/ humane as well as when and how the rest of the psychopaths will strike. Consequently, while many of the texts centre upon the police as a sign of anti-blackness committed by the state, official violence in the texts is consistently compounded by various forms of violence committed by private (white) citizens whose very voices are weaponized to destroy Black people. For Black Americans, these texts argue, the United States is populated by shadowy psychopaths who call them 'nigger' – verbally and/or in their hearts – before calling the police.

In defining the attributes associated with whiteness, Dyer pinpoints enterprise, leadership, and industry among its central features. Defining 'enterprise as an aspect of spirit ... associated with the concept of will' and will as 'the control of self and the control of others' Dyer notes that this value has been central to Western culture since Plato's era.[118] In white Western thinking, 'will' signifies a kind of power as its presence and absence distinguish those who conquer and rule from those who are conquered and ruled.[119] Similarly leadership and enterprise both underpin narratives of human progress as well as proving qualities necessary to push humanity forward. In such Western ideology, 'white people lead humanity forward because of their temperamental

---

[115] Mbembe specifically declares 'The white fears me not at all because of what I have done to it or of what I have given it to see, but owing to what he has done to me and thinks that I could do to him in return'. *Necropolitics*, p. 133.
[116] Mbembe, *Necropolitics*, p. 134.   [117] Mbembe, *Necropolitics*, p. 38.
[118] Dyer, *White*, p. 31.
[119] This construction of 'will' significantly marks whiteness as active and driven, and deserving of freedom as opposed to those who are not willful, or are will-less, and deserving of conquest. Such thinking haunts contemporary racial thought in stereotypes about the laziness of Black populations, evident for instance in the stereotype of the Black welfare Queen. What is laziness if not a lack of will to exert yourself to do anything?

qualities of leadership: will power, far-sightedness, energy'.[120] BLM Gothic texts depict these 'white' qualities as a point of horror and, in doing so, call attention to the ways in which their historic manifestations have been productive of violence. The origin and frontier myths of white America embraces violence as an acceptable aspect of human progress as a kind of regenerative violence. In these myths, violence is satisfying rather than horrifying. The narratives stress 'the sense that an act of violence can sort things out, can raze the world of mess and encumbrances (like intractable land, recalcitrant indigenes, and bad elements within whiteness), can regenerate (a term with such a racial reproductive echo) the land, often by making of the desert a tabula rasa for the establishment of white society'.[121] In contrast BLM Gothic stress the fictional nature of such myths, marking regeneration as limited to and driven by endless white consumption and emphasizing the utterness of the violence while depicting its layered impact.

Get Out best exemplifies BLM Gothic critiques of white enterprise and industry, marking it as contingent upon Black disenfranchisement and as glorifying in Black dehumanization. The film spins around the Armitage family's scientific venture which allows white purchasers to displace the Black psyche and soul with their own. Significantly, the process does not produce a body swap, which would allow the displaced Black person to experience whiteness through bodily occupation. The film marks white industry as productive of a kind of quasi-cannibalistic consumption of Black bodies in white desire to possess Blackness and consume its bodily sensations and experiences. Pliers, Jo's husband in *Destroyer*, also exemplifies BLM Gothic's critiques of white enterprise, leadership, and industry as consumptive and dehumanizing. The text presents the majority of his life through his workplace where he is called only by his nickname 'Pliers'. Importantly, the text never provides his real name, thereby suggesting the absolute dominance the white-led company exercises over his life. They seem to own him and the company leader treats him much like a tool. Eventually, the Director completely erases his humanity as he is forced to pilot and merge with a machine that he can never leave. Pliers literally becomes nothing more than a tool of white leadership, industry, and enterprise.[122]

---

[120] Dyer, *White*, p. 31.

[121] Dyer, *White*, p. 34. Dyer is here building upon Richard Slotkin's influential monograph *Regeneration Through Violence: The Mythology of the American Frontier, 1600–1860*, published in 1973.

[122] Another excellent example from film appears in *The First Purge* (2018), which might be considered a BLM Horror text. The film opens with an interview between the character Skeletor, a Black man, and a white scientist in a completely white room. Skeletor's face bears various tribal-looking scars, his teeth are brown, and his face contorts in fury as he expresses the overwhelming rage that consumes him and his consequent addiction. In contrast, the scientist is

Destroyer further argues that such 'enterprising' traits do not even value other white people as humans but rather sees everyone as a thing to be consumed and/or expelled. A flashback in volume four depicts the Director's conversation with Jo during which she orders Jo to master the secret of immortality. The conversation occurs in virtual reality across various locations, real and imagined. One location is the Creature's body, increased to the size of a landmass. The Director and Jo stand atop his body next to an oilrig drilling into the Creature's flesh. The panel literalizes that which remains implicit in the Director's comments: in capitalist white industry, all life is material to be utilized and consumed, regardless of race. Furthermore, when Jo responds hopefully to the mandate, noting that they could give everyone eternal life, the Director corrects her: 'They don't deserve it. . . . We don't owe them anything. Achievement of your happiness is the only moral purpose of your life'.[123] The text argues that the history of white leadership, enterprise, and industry was never for the benefit of white progress, much less global progress. The Director explains her selfishness as a logical response to general human failures, contending that reckless human behaviour has destroyed the planet. Of course, as the previously described panel reveals, her behaviour repeats the pattern. The text insists that America has always privileged the rights and desires of the elite white individual, and that this value ultimately directs all other white ideals even when it comes at the cost of white lives. The final panel reveals the Director's megalomaniacal aims as she declares that solving the riddle of immortality will make them gods. The Director is at her most grotesque in this moment, her wrinkled face warped as she sits alone on a throne.

The Ballad of Black Tom's Robert Suydam equally destabilizes the aforementioned virtues, marking them as predatory and exploitative even (or especially) when they are done under the pretence of pursuing social justice. Suydam recruits West Indian immigrants from Red Hook to collaborate in his

---

quite pale with light grey hair and very light blue eyes. He remains impassive throughout the interview, picking up on Skeletor's choice of term 'purge' as a suitable term for the program.

While Skeletor seems like the obvious monster, we should rather read the scene as the exchange between Victor Frankenstein and his creation. The scientist not only encourages Skeletor's violence but weaponizes Skeletor's rage and aims it at Skeletor's own, impoverished Black community, thus redirecting it away from the source of Skeletor's actual suffering. The scientist is uncanny in his whiteness, nearly blending with the walls in his pallor and seeming inhuman in his lack of emotion. The opening critiques the very virtues Dyer names as definitive of white authority. The scientist's self-control better enables him to control Skeletor but also proves alienating.

Though Skeletor's violence seems chaotic, the film provides its historical and socioeconomic context. In contrast, the film provides no rationale for the scientist's participation in an experiment that will produce wide-scale violence, chaos, and horror. So then, who is the real monster between the two of them?

[123] LaValle, *Destroyer* vol. 4.

drive to wake the Sleeping King by explaining that, after generations of oppression at the hands of alienating white Americans, people of colour will finally possess the power as supporters of the ancient force. However, Suydam's actual aim is to claim the power entirely for himself as second-in-command to the King. He needs the people of Red Hook to be his willing sacrifices to call the creature. The corrupt white officers are integral to producing the violence and are destroyed in the ritual as well. Much like the Director, Suydam's craving for absolute power consumes all in its path. More importantly, his inherited wealth implies that he is but the most recent installation in a long line of horrifying 'innovators', for Suydam declares 'I know that I am high born. I mean that my family's old wealth, and their bearing in history should afford me all the comfort I need'.[124] Given the nation's origins, the Suydam family's 'old wealth' and 'bearing in history' connects them to an expansionism rooted in racial violence and subjugation as they would have benefited from, if not participated in, the slaughter of the indigenous peoples and the enslavement of Africans.[125] Lastly, Robert Suydam's 'enterprising' conquest is not borne out of necessity but out of boredom, as the comfort he enjoyed began to feel like 'drowning in a child's meal'.[126] The text critiques the horrors white leadership unleashes on populations, marking any 'progress' achieved as incidental to the true aims of the conquest: entertainment and distraction.

'Everybody Dies!' focuses entirely on the connection between anti-Black violence and white entertainment for its horror. All of the guests on Rippa's game show are Black children, thereby recalling the fact that youth and innocence do not save Black people. While Rippa expresses increasing anger, frustration, and sadness at her job – tears running down her face in various segments – a laugh-track accompanies many of the scenes of physical and emotional violence. For example, when made to answer a rigged quiz, the audience laughs every time a child gives the wrong answer. The film stresses the grotesqueness of such 'entertainment' by producing numerous moments of incongruity. When the children enter the stage – victims of a shooting – they enter dancing to the sound of polka music. Like the narrator's vocal intonations, the genre of the musical accompaniment, given its overt associations with Europe, stresses how the moment of Black loss and mourning is a scene of white amusement. Forced to host the show for eternity, Rippa is trapped in

---

[124] LaValle, *Ballad*, p. 49.
[125] Setting the novel in New York does not liberate its characters from association with slavery as Wall Street was the site of one of the largest US slave markets. Slavery was not abolished in the northeast until 1805.
[126] LaValle, *Ballad*, p. 49.

a Black hell. More importantly, it is a hell enjoyed by a whiteness rendered demonic in its amusement and persistence.

The horror extending from anti-Black police violence is just another iteration of a violence which BLM Gothic critiques as endemic to whiteness historically. The violence of the police in BLM Gothic (and reality) must be understood as an extension of an enterprising whiteness which readily embraces violence as 'regenerative' and masks the resultant horror as a virtue. The white officers' recurrent harassment of Tommy in *The Ballad of Black Tom* particularly rejects the notion of police violence as anything but a form of brutal terror: 'Tommy waited before reaching down for his guitar case. No sudden moves in front of even a sullen cop. Just because Malone wasn't as rough as the private detective didn't mean he was gentle'.[127] Early in the plot, officers descend to the level of a dangerous animal that must be approached carefully. The text essentially reduces white Americans to beasts in describing the horror and threat they pose to unsuspecting Black people. Later Malone further descends from the place of the human, looking up at Tommy's arrival 'as if he'd been sensitive to Tester's scent'.[128] The implicit metaphor becomes explicit later, accompanying the shift in their violence: 'he saw the patrol cars parked in the middle of the road like three great black hounds waiting to pounce on all these gathered sheep'.[129] As much as the populace has been reduced to the level of the subhuman, so too have their tormentors become malicious hounds slavering to consume their prey. Their violence becomes like the bark and bite of a dog as the officers weaponize terror and surprise. The inevitable result of such behaviour is a grotesque level of personal violence when one officer shoots Tommy's sleeping father Otis.[130] As if to stress the irrationality of the crime, Howard quips 'I felt in danger for my life .... I emptied my revolver. Then I reloaded and did it again'.[131] The violence, which would be recuperated as 'regenerative' in Frontier narratives, is revealed to be little more than a base (and debasing) craving for Black suffering and death.

Likewise Burke, recalling his encounter with Sherman, notes that he saw 'the real face of fear' on Sherman's face as the mob of officers approached the room (Figure 8). Yet such chaotic violence extends beyond law enforcement to private citizens acting in semi-official roles. The perpetrator in 'Haint in the Window' for example is a white security guard named Rick. Like the officers, Rick proves a source of discomfort and apprehension to Darryl, who suffers a knot in his stomach after their first encounter. Like the officers in *The Ballad of Black Tom*, Rick's humanity diminishes throughout the story. For instance, Rick attempts to

---

[127] LaValle, *Ballad*, p. 25. [128] LaValle, *Ballad*, p. 61. [129] LaValle, *Ballad*, p. 66.
[130] LaValle, *Ballad*, p. 82. [131] LaValle, *Ballad*, p. 82.

Figure 8 Sherman, frightened by the sound of approaching officers

intimidate Darryl while wearing a uniform that makes him look like an SS officer.¹³² The uniform predicts the same craving for violence that Howard reveals in shooting Tommy's father. Later Rick reappears, 'amped up on imagination and anger when he turned the corner, his gun already drawn, looking for something to shoot'.¹³³ Invariably, Rick shoots Darryl in his own store, acting in a semi-official capacity as a local security guard. Rick's position is important given that he is not sanctioned by state or federal government to act in such a death-dealing capacity. The story, like other BLM Gothic texts, reminds us that, in a country of heavily-armed white citizens taught to devalue Black life, any individual can exercise violent anti-Blackness with a similar level of sanctioning.¹³⁴

The texts repeatedly reveal that Black subjects must embrace and perform invisibility just to survive the onslaught of white antagonism. Yet this embrace and performance also renders Black people complicit in their dehumanization and erasure. bell hooks, for instance, in speaking about this tactic observes how 'black people learned to appear before whites as though they were zombies, cultivating the habit of casting the gaze downward so as not to appear uppity. To look directly was an assertion of subjectivity, equality. Safety resides in the pretence of invisibility'.¹³⁵ On refusing to look, Black citizens not only surrender their

---

¹³² Due, 'The Haint', p. 33.   ¹³³ Due, 'The Haint', p. 48.
¹³⁴ There have been a number of unjustified shootings of unarmed Black men by white citizens who have proclaimed themselves 'security' agents. Consider for instance, Ahmaud Arbery's killers, who confronted and restrained Arbery though they were private citizens.
¹³⁵ hooks, *Black Looks*, p. 168.

subjectivity and claims to equality, they also surrender their claims to humanity by positioning themselves as 'zombies' amidst a hostile white population. Tommy particularly exemplifies this practice and the surrender it constitutes. Explaining that 'Becoming unremarkable, invisible, compliant... were useful tricks for a black man in an all-white neighbourhood. Survival techniques'[136] Tommy attempts to claim agency in the performance, marking the invisibility as a 'trick'. Yet shortly thereafter Tommy describes this performance revealingly as 'His foot-shuffling technique'.[137] While it may seem a minor description, 'foot-shuffling' alludes back to stereotypes of Black people as bumbling and lazy 'coons', a stereotype popular on vaudeville stages in the late nineteenth century and later reinvigorated in early twentieth-century cinema by Stepin Fetchit. Like the original 'coon' caricature, Stepin Fetchit's character was inarticulate, slack-jawed, and slow-witted; he walked and talked as slowly as he thought. The foot-shuffle references these horrible stereotypes and caricatures of Black people as perpetually lethargic and intellectually dense. The horror of adopting the performance does not end at the soul-crushing embrace of a humiliating caricature.[138] In fact, the stereotype had very real consequences as whites used them to rationalize continued Black disenfranchisement and oppression. One white writer, for example, explained that newly emancipated Black people were 'lazy, thriftless, intemperate, insolent, dishonest, and without the most rudimentary elements of morality. ..... Universally, they report a general depravity and retrogression of the Negroes at large in sections in which they are left to themselves, closely resembling a reversion to barbarism'.[139] Therefore, Tommy's performance, while mandated by white violence as a method of Black survival, also contributes to the very anti-Black ideologies behind white antagonism. Whiteness ensnares Tommy in a psychological and emotional iteration of the Gothic escape-capture cycle.[140]

Perhaps most troubling of all, otherwise nurturing Black spaces transform into horrifying locales in the presence of questionable, if not outright oppressive, white Americans. In doing so, BLM Gothic reverses the spectre of Black intrusion in white spaces as a point of horror, apparent in films like the original *Candyman* (1992) and, as Robin Means Coleman explains, in political ads like George H.W. Bush's 'infamous Willie Horton political ad

---

[136] LaValle, *Ballad*, p. 12.   [137] LaValle, *Ballad*, p. 13.
[138] The text points to the level of psychological devastation that accompanies this self-effacement, noting the shuffle replaces the 'lion's stride' which Black men possessed in their own neighborhoods and among their own communities. LaValle, *Ballad*, p. 12.
[139] Page, *The Negro*, p. 80.
[140] We might connect this question of Black performativity pursued for survival back to Richard Wright's 'The Ethics of Living Jim Crow' (1940) in which he provides an overview of the humiliations and dangers Black people face from white citizens during the Jim Crow era. His essay ends with a similar, challenging performance. See Wright, 'The Ethics of Living Jim Crow', p. 15.

campaign'.[141] These transformations are especially nightmarish as all-Black locations can function as 'safe spaces', restive places where Blacks can freely explore and critique the sociopolitical issues confronting them; as places that empower Blacks and where they can pause to recuperate in fights for social justice.[142] White intrusion into such locations constitutes a threat to Black peace. For example, the presence of the white police force transforms Harlem for Tommy. As noted in the previous section, Harlem is the haven Tommy longs for when he is away from it; the mere presence of the white officers transforms Harlem for Tommy and he looks 'with new eyes' at the decaying façade of his tenement. Harlem shifts from being a beloved haven to a rundown ghetto when intruded upon by hostile whites. Darryl similarly mourns the transformation of his Black bookstore Sankofa as affluent and well-meaning whites displace the former Black residents during the area's gentrification. Reflecting on the 1992 Los Angeles riots, Darryl recalls how

> the strip mall across the street had gone up in flames while Mrs. Richardson opened her doors to anyone who needed to sob or rant, or both, behind the safety of her bookshelves. Fruit of Islam guarded the doors, but even if they hadn't, Darryl's father and his Uncle Boo–both high school football coaches– would have joined any dozen other men or women to protect Sankofa and its treasures. Smoke rose east, west, north, and south of Sankofa, but not a single page in the bookstore burned.[143]

The communal protection of the store signals its importance to the population as a place of exchange and recuperation for Black people despite their other differences. It was the only place Black residents could come to wrestle with the trauma arising out of the Rodney King verdict, when the court proclaimed that a Black man's life was worth less than a dog's. Yet the soul of the bookstore slowly dies in the face of gentrification; the store might remain but the safety it offered to Black visitors is lost, replaced instead by an atmosphere suggestive of a Barnes & Noble.

Such problematic intrusions prove outright destructive in the midst of a violently anti-Black climate. While officers' intrusion into Harlem initially results only in psychological violence, the white police force eventually turns Harlem into an outright war zone. Similarly, Jo's own cabin home in *Destroyer* becomes a literal battleground as two white agents invade her space. The text stresses the transformation of the cabin from haven to battle zone by juxtaposing

---

[141] Similar to *Candyman* (1992), the ad's message centred upon the threat of Black men intruding in white spaces to rape white women. Means Coleman, *Horror Noire*, p. 147.

[142] The notion of the 'safe space' is one that is particularly defined and prized in Black Feminism. It was first defined by Patricia Hill Collins in *Black Feminist Thought: Knowledge, Consciousness and the Politics of Empowerment* (2000).

[143] Due, 'The Haint', pp. 37–38.

scenes of the cabin's decorations – including numerous pictures of Akai at various ages, and of Jo and Pliers in a loving embrace – with the scenes of the white agents' examinations of Jo's possessions and the dialogue between the cabin's sentient defence system and Jo. As the agents rummage through her home, Jo remarks that 'it's safer to let them think they've accomplished something. Powerlessness makes a man more likely to use his gun'.[144] The comment suggests that her safety depends upon performing vulnerability at their invasion because the men will become even more deadly if she does not. Notably, sensing her awareness of their presence, Byron and Percy draw their guns before descending into her basement lab, despite orders to return with Jo alive. Upon finding her, the agents open fire, shooting Jo eighteen times. The Black home/haven becomes a place not just of vulnerability but of death in the face of white incursion. Such scenes are reflective of actual events as a number of Black victims were shot unarmed in their own homes.[145] Furthermore, Jo humorously quips that they are in a 'stand your ground' state, thereby hinting at her right to armed self-defence. The agents' response – opening fire – signals their and the text's awareness of who has the right to stand their, versus take others', ground.

BLM Gothic texts clarify how it is that white Americans prove more nightmarish and horrifying than a Lovecraftian monster by connecting their institutional dominance and the whiteness of American hegemony to a very base need: insatiable hunger. BLM Gothic argues that the rationale for anti-Black violence is ultimately white craving for Black suffering. As previously noted, *The Ballad of Black Tom* reduces the white officers to slavering dogs 'waiting to pounce on ... sheep',[146] but the sheep are, of course, other people. The excessive nature of Howard's murder of Otis – the reason the officers have cordoned off the neighbourhood – further comments on the excess of the officers' hunger for Black suffering. Just as Howard is driven to reload and fire more shots into the aged and unarmed man, so too are the officers outside over-eager to accost and forcefully detain passers-by. Such hunger ends in the absurd siege on Harlem in which the officers turn weapons of war upon an American city and its (non-white) population. Darryl is similarly the victim of an insatiable hunger that results in his violent death in 'The Haint in the Window'. Like Howard, security guard Rick shoots Darryl more than once. Unlike LaValle's novella, Due's story refuses to specify the number of times Rick shoots Darryl, marking only the first

---

[144] LaValle, *Destroyer* vol. 1.
[145] See, for example, Sonya Massey who was shot by the very police she called for protection; Atatiana Jefferson who was with her eight-year-old nephew when police shot her through her house's window; and Botham Jean who was sitting on his sofa eating ice cream when an officer entered his home and shot him.
[146] LaValle, *Ballad*, p. 66.

gunshot. The refusal to specify suggests excess while also marking the first shot fired as an excess itself. The text warns of the concluding violence and of the white cannibalistic cravings early on, connecting the two:

> Darryl knew this particular man ... was a security guard because he couldn't qualify for LAPD, which was a true testament to his instability. And he deeply craved an excuse to hurt a smartass like Darryl Martin Jones. To kill someone, if he could get away with it–just to see what it might feel like. Even his smile looked like a trap ready to spring.[147]

Through marking Rick as too unstable even for the Los Angeles Police Department, the text first reflects on the pervasiveness of white hunger for Black suffering, as the LAPD will, the text implies, generally accept officers with a craving for violence. While Rick proves too unstable to be a police officer, he is nonetheless a typical white citizen. Darryl easily recognizes him as the type of person who longs to kill someone like Darryl – a Black man who speaks (or rather, quips) back. Lastly, the story implicitly connects the violence to cannibalistic consumption by stressing Rick's mouth as a point of danger. Like the officers in Tommy's Harlem, Rick is slavering for Darryl's death.

The films similarly stress whiteness as cannibalistic in its consumption of Black spaces, suffering and bodies. For example, *Get Out* (2017) plays upon the idea of white sociopolitical and cultural appropriations of Black bodies, culture, and artefacts as the superficial Black skin is consumed by a white subject while the mind, heart, and soul of the body is tossed aside as waste. The phrase 'a mind is a terrible thing to waste' proves the haunting quip throughout the film, as that is exactly what the white characters are doing. Similarly, the art critic Finley Stephens changes her mind about Anthony's installation only after his work is connected to the death of the gallery curator in *Candyman*. While Finley's explanation that the story of the curator's death makes Anthony's installation valuable would seem to focus solely on the consumption of white suffering, Finley's interview with Anthony teases out his traumatic experience as well as the violence suffered by Black communities. Finley remarks

> Your work is so macabre and that's pretty interesting considering what happened. .... I'm not saying that you're at fault. And I'm certainly not saying that a ghost manifested by collective storytelling killed a prominent art dealer. I'm just saying that all of a sudden your work seems ... eternal. What's next?[148]

Anthony's installation is, of course, a retelling of the Candyman legend. Finley's comments, while superficially eschewing any connections between the murder

---

[147] Due, 'The Haint', p. 34.   [148] *Candyman* (2021).

and Anthony, nevertheless reveal a desire to consume more narratives of Black suffering – given Candyman's origins – and vengeful rage.

That we are meant to read Finley's interest as another form of white cannibalism becomes apparent when Anthony lectures her on white creation, suffocation, and consumption of Black ghettos. Notably, the original extended version of the scene makes clear its point about the connection between gentrification, art consumption, and white cannibalism of suffering Black bodies:

> Who do you think makes the hood? The city cuts off a community and waits for it to die. It waits, like a vulture, for the roads to be addled with potholes, for buildings to crumble, for crime to rise ... for desperation to lead to broken homes and broken spirits. It waits for it all to be unlivable, for everyone in it to feel hopeless. Then they invite developers in, to find some derelict building, do the bare minimum on the façade, and say 'hey you artists, you young people, you white, preferably or only, please come to the hood, it's cheap. And here's your white-tiled black grouted café for you; they won't dare come in here. And if you stick it out for a couple of years, we'll bring you a Whole Foods.[149]

The extended scene, included in the DVD version of the film, explicitly marks white systemic and structural anti-Blackness as a kind of cannibalism that particularly relishes Black physical, emotional, and spiritual deprivation and ruination. The extended lecture clarifies the number of ways whites 'consume' Blacks for pleasure as even the remnants of Blackness reappear as the ground-down material, grout, linking seemingly disconnected whiteness. The starving, liberal white artist, as one tile among many, is brought into the structure of white dominance in line with other iterations of whiteness through the promise of keeping Blacks out. Black death, through stagnation and its perpetual disenfranchisement and marginalization in white definitions of humanity and citizenship, serves to recuperate a whiteness which might otherwise reject the centre. That whites also suffer in this dynamic – as murder victim and as unwitting purchaser of a shoddy product – only further dehumanizes the practitioners, who happily consume all.[150]

---

[149] *Candyman* (2021).
[150] BLM Gothic is certainly not the first mode to approach issues of white consumptions of Black culture and bodies. For instance, bell hooks's monograph *Black Looks: Race and Representation* deals intimately with white consumption of otherness in a chapter called 'Eating the Other'. There she teases out the dehumanizing aspects of white consumptive practice, noting how white American culture picks apart the Black text and/or cultural element – like language, fashion and music – to make it readily palatable for white consumption by emptying it of its cultural and historical meaning, which are defined as so much detritus (or excrement, in keeping with the metaphor of 'eating'). Audre Lorde similarly comments on the politics of racial and gendered appropriation in 'Age, Race, Class, and Sex: Women Redefining Difference'.

Inevitably predominantly white locales prove places of inherent terror in BLM Gothic. Terming the spaces Whitopia's,[151] Robin Means Coleman and Novotny Lawrence explain how films like *Get Out* turn these locales into something which is simultaneously monstrous in their 'terrifying *violation of cultural and economic boundaries*' and 'quintessential[ly] *"everyday"*'.[152] [italic in the original] A response to the dangerous Black ghettos that dominated Horror films for much of the twentieth century, Whitopias are places of risk, terror, and destruction for Black people in BLM Gothic. For example, although Darryl's neighbourhood was initially occupied by a Black community, he feels alienated now that the region has been gentrified and is predominantly white. Remarking that 'he already didn't recognize the rest of the street', Darryl complains that 'his new customers wanted to treat him like a Barnes & Noble'.[153] Importantly, the text's phrasing displaces the bookstore, Sankofa, with Darryl's own body, implying that he has been reduced to a dehumanized point of consumption and service. Tommy Tester's journeys into the suburban Whitopia of New York city are even more fraught and terrifying. When Tommy initially declares that 'he'd be going out to Flatbush, in the middle of the night, into the home of a white man', Otis expresses terror as Tommy 'might as well have told his father he planned to go wrestle a bear'.[154] Otis understandably responds 'I don't care if you've got to spill blood to do it, but you get out of that house at the end of the job and you get back to me'.[155] Otis's extreme terror and anxiety over Tommy's journey and his emphatic insistence that Tommy survive at all costs render the Whitopia a trap occupied by inhuman predators. The Black citizen journeying to such places must be prepared to fight to the death to escape.

The beginning of *Get Out* specifically addresses the danger of the Whitopia as Andre, a Black man, travels through a middle-class white suburb. Speaking to a friend on the phone as he walks, Andre proclaims himself lost in a hedge-maze, alluding to the hedge maze in Stanley Kubrick's film rendition of Stephen King's novel *The Shining*. Kubrick's/King's hedge maze is hyperwhite (Figure 9) as it is covered in snow and a place of horrible domestic violence as an axe-wielding Jack Torrence pursues his child Danny through the labyrinth. Like Danny, Andre must use his wits to survive the maze and thereby acts decisively when a white car (Figure 10) – alluding to the snowy whiteness of the actual maze – begins to follow him. Unlike Danny, wits do not save Andre. The

---

[151] Means Coleman and Lawrence borrow the term from Rich Benjamin's *Searching for Whitopia: An Improbable Journey into the Heart of White America*. Notably, Whitopia's typically present themselves as ordinary, friendly, orderly, safe and comfortable. See Means Coleman, Robin, *Horror Noire*.
[152] Means Coleman and Lawrence, 'A Peaceful Place', p. 47.
[153] Due, 'The Haint', pp. 37, 36.   [154] LaValle, *Ballad*, pp. 32–33.
[155] LaValle, *Ballad*, p. 35.

Figure 9 The snow covered hedge maze through which axe-wielding Jack Torrence chases his son

Figure 10 Andre walking through a Whitopia, another kind of dangerous white hedge maze

scene performs BLM Gothic anxieties about whiteness, location, and ownership, revealing how Black 'anxieties [are] about the people who "own" the land. For they are the ones who enslaved, brutalized, and exploited Blacks (and other people of color) with the distinct goal of profiting off of the crops produced on "their" property'.[156] In BLM Gothic, whites continue to consume and profit from Black people who are treated as property to be claimed and dispensed at white leisure. The texts point to the horrific history underpinning Whitopias and mark the ways they remain traps to ensnare even wary Black travelers. Whereas white-centred Horror films of the late twentieth-century marked the Black urban area as one in which 'the innocent, those who could not get out, were held hostage',[157] BLM Gothic marks Whitopias as spaces in which innocent Blacks cannot get out and are not only held hostage but consumed and destroyed.

Even the journey to the Whitopia is fraught with perils for Black characters. As a dehumanized subject, Tommy suffers excessive surveillance on the train ride to the suburb as white men ask him four different times about his destination. These implicit threats become explicit once Tommy arrives at Suydam's locality and dares to leave the train. Leaving the station, three white males pursue Tommy, trying to intimidate him in a manner similar to the behavior of the white police in Harlem. Finally outrunning them and making it to Sudyam's property, Tommy turns to realize that the 'boys were younger than him. Maybe fifteen or sixteen. Children'.[158] The scene recasts the violent deaths of innocent unarmed Black children with a number of important differences. While, as

---

[156] Means Coleman and Lawrence, 'A Peaceful Place', p. 61.
[157] Means Coleman, *Horror Noire*, p. 175.   [158] LaValle, *Ballad,* p. 38.

Section 1 noted, Black youth are unseen and denied their innocence by being recast as monsters, these white children act monstrous. Where Black children like Tamir Rice and his fictional double Jerome are murdered for playing with a harmless toy, the white boys pose an actual threat to Tommy as they outnumber him, chase him, and promise to assault him if they catch him. Indeed, the boys' whiteness enables them to do actual harm to the older Black youth, if not by sanctioned physical force, then through the exercise of their voices.

Atticus's journey, along with his friend and uncle, to white-dominated Ardham in *Lovecraft Country* provides the series' entrance into the Gothic while reiterating the journey to and through Whitopia as hazardous to Black life. In the episode titled 'Sundown' the series alludes to the actual violence African Americans confronted when traveling through white areas. For instance, stopping at a café that they believed to be safe for Black customers because it is listed in the Green Book,[159] the group find themselves in their first snare. As in the traditional Gothic, Atticus and friends must interpret various minute details in order to accurately read the location, barely becoming cognizant of the danger they are in before fleeing the café while pursued by a carload of armed, hollering white men. Pausing to rest in the woods after their escape, the soundtrack again signals danger as a patrol car slowly pulls up behind them. The white officer invariably informs them that they are in a sundown town and need to make it across the border or else face violence (Figure 11). As the officer follows them in his car, the group must find a way to make it across the line without speeding or else they will still face grave consequences (Figure 12). White locations are presented as cruel traps in which Blacks face a recurrent escape-capture cycle that leads them, ultimately, only to more horror at the end of the line. Reaching Ardham does not provide safety for the group either. Escorted into the village after their rescue from the officers, the place proves uncanny both in its atmosphere and in the semi-religious behaviour and speech of its residents. Of course, Atticus has been summoned to be a sacrifice for the elite men rulers the town. In the Whitopia, Blacks become the mice to sadistic white cats.

In each case, the white-dominated location is a place of hyper-surveillance as Black subjects are overly seen for their difference but not for their humanity. Tommy, in planning his second trip to Suydam's mansion, details the hazards and horrors of the white region:

> A Negro walking through this white neighborhood at damn near midnight? He might as well be Satan strolling through Eden. And if they found him with

---

[159] This is based on an actual publication titled *The Negro Motorist Green Book*, a guidebook released annually for Black roadtrippers. Published by Victor Hugo Green, the book listed businesses such as hotels, restaurants, and gas stations that were relatively friendly to African Americans.

African American Gothic

Figure 11 A white officer threatens Atticus and friends to get out of town before sunset

Figure 12 Leti watches in terror as they are pursued by the white officer

that wad of money, well, he'd be fortunate if the police were called. They might only beat him, then take him to jail. Much worse would happen if he got snatched by a mob.[160]

Tommy does not imagine what violence might await him, alluding to its excess only in terms of the protection that will be denied to him. The horrific violence proves literally unquantifiable as even the initial implicit harm is exponentially multiplied in the face of multiple antagonists. As much as racist fantasy reduces Blacks violators of white peace and sanctity to the realm of monstrosity, this racist ideology is productive of a very real violence that is so horrible it defies speech. The locations offer violence on multiple levels as Black subjects suffer visual surveillance suggestive of containment, and psychological and emotional violence before any actual attack ever occurs.[161] As Tommy concludes, by travelling to a white area he might as well 'travel to another universe'.[162] Like the intergalactic traveler, a Black American making such journeys is enveloped in an unending blackness and utterly isolated, left to face new dangers with each step.

'Everybody Dies!' marks the white space as unavoidable and inescapable, thereby alluding to an implicit concern of BLM Gothic texts – there is no avoiding, much less escaping, violating interracial encounters. As citizens in

---

[160] LaValle, *Ballad*, p. 45.
[161] BLM Gothic's portrayal of white surveillance of Black people is quite similar to Foucault's iteration of the panopticon and its functioning. Unable to fully identify if and when they are being surveilled, Blacks must assume they are always being watched.
[162] LaValle, *Ballad*, p. 35.

a white-dominated, governed, and legislated country, Blacks must make such forays into white locations daily as the entirety of the nation falls under the claim and control of whiteness. Even when there are no white people present, it remains a white-governed space, as we see in the game show stage of Bodomo's film. That there is no power for Blacks within this space is evident in the Reaper's numerous failed attempts at resistance and escape. For instance, when Rippa snatches the earpiece from her head to angrily list the various ways Blacks are unjustly murdered before ending in the rhyme 'kids beware when they attack, 'specially if you are Black',[163] the scene drops and the show is briefly replaced by a 'technical difficulties' card. When Rippa begins to read the story of one child who pleads for salvation, the white narrator interrupts the scene declaring 'it's not your turn yet'.[164] That there is no hope for Blacks in this space is especially apparent in the quiz segment in which the children/guests are tasked with providing answers to an unasked question. They each provide the wrong answer, unsurprisingly, and Rippa finally explains that 'death is the only answer'.[165] Finally tired of her job, Rippa decides to leave the stage and attempts to exit through the death door herself. All the while the white narrator continues to announce the next week's guests and events, pausing each time Rippa leaves the stage and resuming upon her reappearance. The white-created and governed space becomes a prison of terror, pain, and death even for what should be the most powerful figure of all: death, when death is Black.

3 Becoming the Monster

Angry is good. Angry get's ... shit ... done.[166]

Like Mary Shelley, I would tell the story of a mother who lost her child far too soon.... she would bring back the dead from across the veil. But, of course, even this would not bring her peace. She would create life, but she would use that creation for vengeance. Her grief and rage would inspire only one goal: destroy.[167]

Black rage is a bottomless pit. It has no real destination. And whatever comes out of that on the ground is more explosive and more frightening than anything else.[168]

In the episode 'Goatman' from the Black Horror podcast *Run, Fool!* writer and presenter Rodney Barnes tells the story of a Goatman haunting (and hunting in) Prince George's County, Maryland.

---

[163] 'Everybody Dies!' [164] 'Everybody Dies!' [165] 'Everybody Dies!'
[166] *American Gods*, 'The Secret of Spoons'. [167] LaValle, *Destroyer* 6 vols.
[168] Park, 'Afropessimism and Futures of ... ', p. 40.

Barnes explains that the story began generations earlier with a Black goat farmer named Mr Wilson, someone described as 'one of the kindest, gentlest men' who 'had a smile for everyone who visited his farm, and kept the happiest, best fed animals you'd ever seen. He also happened to be the only Black man in town'.[169] Wilson kept to himself and would walk to town every Sunday selling milk, cheese, and produce. Over time Wilson began appearing with fewer offerings, looking tired and 'without a trace of the big smile he usually wore'.[170] It turns out people in the town had begun to turn on Wilson, resenting him for making money off of them when he was a Black man and they were white. The townspeople began by slaughtering his livestock slowly. Once they had killed all of his animals, they targeted Wilson himself, arriving one night hidden under cover of darkness to hang him from a bridge. Soon after their animals, especially dogs, were slaughtered on that same bridge. The story then shifts to a slightly later era, when a pair of teenage twins decides to play a gruesome prank on another child. Like the townspeople and Wilson, the twin boys resented their classmate for failing to show them proper respect. The prank results in all of their deaths. The Goatman slaughters the twin's victim during the prank. When the twins realize what they have done, they return to hunt the creature under cover of darkness with their dog only to meet their deaths as well. Barnes concludes the episode by explaining

> I think about the Goatman too. . . . . I don't stay up at night thinking about the creature itself. I'm more bothered about how he got there. See the story of Mr. Wilson is about a group of folks who didn't think he deserved success just because of the color of his skin, pure and simple. And thinking you're better than someone else and punishing them for it . . . well, that's also an everybody problem. . . . . And though headlights and sodium lamps and what have you might keep away the Goatman, it will do nothing for the problem that made him. And that, my friends, is just as important to watch out for as the lethal monster that stalks the woods of Prince Georges County.[171]

I begin this section here because of how the podcast episode perfectly illustrates one of the primary horrors of BLM Gothic: the seeming inevitability of Black turns to monstrous violence in response to profoundly violent anti-Blackness. As implied in Barnes's story, part of the turn to monstrosity is a justified and logical anger arising out of the uncanny repetition of anti-Black violence across generations. In the story, the twin's prank on their victim reproduces the

---

[169] Barnes, 'The Goatman'.   [170] Barnes, 'The Goatman'.   [171] Barnes, 'The Goatman'.

elements of Wilson's murder; they perfectly repeat history when they arrive to hunt the Goatman. Like the lynch mob, the twins arrived armed with shotguns and a dog, and turn off their car's headlights to do further violence. The story's arc illustrates the ways contemporary anti-Blackness re-enacts previous eras of lynching. Wilson's transformation into a violent, angry creature is understandable. Yet equally important in the story, and to this section, are the victims.

Like the podcast episode, BLM Gothic depicts how Blacks in the twenty-first century have vented a justified rage in the wake of continued assaults on unarmed, sometimes adolescent, Blacks. Acknowledging the long history of Black dehumanization and the failures of numerous attempts to argue for equality and social justice through civil and legal methods, BLM Gothic argues that the resulting frustration, despair and anger produces a logical outburst of wrath which, decontextualized, is easily coded as 'monstrous' even when the violence is necessitated by racist assaults. Such protagonists might be read as 'willful monsters' in Natalie Wilson's articulation of the theory, although the conclusions of BLM Gothic text challenge the issue of choice implicit in Wilson's theory. Black protagonists encounter the figurative and literal walls erected by an oppressive and dominating society, and breach – if not utterly eradicate – the barriers. In their assault on oppressive systems and the people that maintain them, these figures issue a challenge to the 'general will' and 'destabilize meaning, [and] threaten to erode hierarchies'.[172] While logically these are clearly heroic acts of violence, the very act of the margin(alized) assaulting the centre becomes a point of horror and monstrosity.

The texts present an array of protagonists engaging in radical violence. Some are vengeful Black protagonists easily subsumed by the idea of the monstrous – their cries of injustice diminished beneath the horror of their uncontrolled outrage. Others convey a focused rage and retain some of their sympathetic aspects. Importantly, while the texts understand the shifts, they mourn rather than laud the need for violence even when controlled. The texts iterate the power and implicit terror in Frank Wilderson's comments (the third epigraph) to reveal their place within Afropessimism. The characters consistently burn worlds to the ground. Yet the casualties suffered in the radical act also recall Mbembe's warning that while 'regenerative violence [may be] aimed to produce other forms of life .... Set loose, it [is] liable to become uncontrollable'.[173]

The ghost in 'The Haint in the Window' metaphorically raises the question of embracing a behaviour which might be read as monstrous, tossing the theoretical books by UCLA professors aside to replace them instead with Frantz Fanons' *The Wretched of the Earth* and *The Autobiography of Malcolm X*.[174] The references are telling. American history demonizes Malcolm X, presenting him as the dark alter to

---

[172] Wilson, *Willful Monsters*, p. 10.   [173] Mbembe, *Necropolitics*, p. 129.
[174] Due, 'The Haint', pp. 35–36.

Reverend Dr Martin Luther King, who (white) Americans valorize for his insistence on non-violence.[175] The turn to Fanon's text is even more telling given the work's expressions of violence. Noting that Fanon envisions radical decolonization in the text through violent labour, Mbembe stresses the destructive elements of Fanon's argument, wondering 'does all violence create something new? What about the sorts of violence that found nothing, on which nothing can be founded, and whose unique function is to institute disorder, chaos, and loss?'[176] The trajectory of Fanon's work reveals a similar path to revolution that BLM Gothic argues is inevitable; his first text *Black Skin White Masks* (1952) approaches anti-Blackness from the place of theory and rhetoric, asking questions and presenting wounds in a fashion that also stressed Fanon's civility. *Wretched of the Earth*, while still exploring the psychological costs of racial oppression, interrogates the uses of 'regenerative violence' in the fight for social justice. Some white Americans saw the text as a source of terror as groups like the Black Panthers and figures such as Stokely Carmichael deemed the book essential reading.[177] Indeed, one writer for *The New Yorker* claimed in 1966 that 'Fanon's "arguments for violence" are "spreading amongst the young Negroes in American slums"'[178] thereby hinting that a horrifying wave of anti-white violence was brewing, and would be carried out by America's most alien(ated) populace. Like Due's story, other BLM Gothic texts recognize this historical precedent to reveal the recent outrage and consequent violence as an inevitable, logical though undesirable turn, even as these eruptions make Blacks easy targets for claims of monstrosity.

As noted in Section 2, there are various forms of monstrosity, but violence is a characteristic of them all. Indeed, Weinstock lists 'vengeful nature' as one kind of monstrosity. Vengeance turns nature into a thing of terror. Likewise, vengeful outlash is one of the forms of monstrosity which BLM Gothic mourns as inevitable in a population that has endured generations of necropolitical assault. Ruby in *Lovecraft Country* and Burke in *Candyman* exemplify this form of monstrosity. Ruby enacts vengeance on her white manager, who she witnesses molesting another Black sales clerk. Disguised as a white woman, Ruby lures the manager into a secluded office and then proceeds to sexually assault him. Her attack is

---

[175] Of course, these American memorialization of the two figures simplifies and misrepresents the two men, especially King, who was considered an enemy of the state by the FBI. Towards the end of his life, King began to reconsider if non-violence was the most effective way to achieve racial equality.

[176] Mbembe, *Necropolitics*, p. 118.

[177] The Black Panthers were notorious for embracing violence in defending themselves and their community, appearing in pictures carrying guns openly. Stockley Carmichael was initially part of the nonviolent group SNCC but later left the group, became more militant, and joined the Black Panthers. FBI director J. Edgar Hoover identified Carmichael as the successor to Malcolm X.

[178] Mishra, 'Frantz Fanon's Enduring Legacy'.

Figure 13 Ruby transforming back into her Black body while attacking her manager

Figure 14 Burke forcing Anthony to become Candyman

especially brutal as she mounts her employer, forcefully and repeatedly thrusting the heel of her stiletto into his rear. The excessiveness of her assault suggests she is unleashing repressed rage against more than just that one man. Furthermore, in the midst of her outlash, Ruby transforms back into her Black body – the white flesh melts away from her, dropping off in bloody clumps, leaving Ruby heaving, panting and covered in blood (atop her victim (Figure 13). The mid-rape transformation calls attention to the monstrosity of her rage and actions when we might otherwise be tempted to applaud Ruby as rape and racism avenger.

Although Burke is not as visually grotesque as Ruby, he too becomes a monster in his violent outlash and consequent assault on Anthony in his attempt to create a Candyman that is weaponized and targeted at the white community to kill 'their fathers, their babies, their sisters'. Having kidnapped Anthony, Burke calls police officers to the scene knowing they will immediately fire upon and kill his victim. While Burke does not undergo a supernatural shift in his appearance, his face twitches and contorts in grotesque ways, his body out of control just as he is psychologically and emotionally out of control (Figure 14), thereby rendering him 'monster'. Further, we might read him as similar to Victor Frankenstein given that Burke also seeks to create a monster;[179] Anthony's deformed and grotesque body may be read as an extension of Burke's face. Like Ruby, Burke's rage extends beyond the victim he is busy brutalizing.

Tommy in *The Ballad of Black Tom* best exemplifies the shift to monstrosity that arises out of Black rage. As noted in Section 1, the novel changes in its referent for the protagonist: Tommy, the sweet and naïve young man, becomes Black Tom halfway through the text after the murder of his father. Tommy's name change

---

[179] Where Victor pulls body parts together to create his Creature, Burke dismantles bits of Anthony's body, sawing off Anthony's hand and forcing a hook into the bloody stump.

accommodates other shifts as Tommy assumes a shadowy, menacing and mythic aspect. Malone, upon encountering Black Tom, observes how 'His demeanor, even his voice, was greatly changed from when they'd last met'.[180] Later the text explicitly comments on the changes, thereby marking Black Tom a point of horror:

> "I bear a hell within me," Black Tom growled. "And finding myself unsympathized with, wished to tear up the trees, spread havoc and destruction around me, and then to have sat down and enjoyed the ruin."
> "You're a monster, then," Malone said.
> "I was made one."[181]

Black Tom growls during the exchange, descending into the same beastliness which defines the inhuman(e) white officers. The exchange also recalls exchanges between Frankenstein and his Creature as Black Tom, like the Creature, explains that his rage originates in the injustices he has been forced to bear alone. Yet while their monstrosity has been pressed upon them by self-righteous and entitled creators, Black Tom and the Creature are still both inhuman(e), even though they are justified in their rage.

This shift towards monstrosity also occurs alongside another narrative shift as Tommy loses his individuation and is more frequently referred to as 'the Negro' in the second half of the text. The shift to the term 'negro' alludes to the history of white dehumanization of Black people and the will to mark them as subhuman. In aligning the term with Tommy's behavioural shift, the novella implies that Black Tom has become the kind of monster whiteness always predetermined him to be. Significantly, white stereotypes of Black people as subhuman depict Blacks as unfeeling, wild and unloving. Black people were supposedly resistant to physical pain, hypersexual, violent towards each other and emotionally detached. While Tommy as Black Tom does not fulfil all of these stereotypes about Black subhumanity, he does reproduce the most violent among them. The climax of the novella occurs as the police siege a block in Tommy's neighbourhood. As the officers' machine guns demolish the apartment buildings despite the screaming, innocent tenants still inside, Black Tom revels in the chaos and pain, claiming it as a song all his own.[182] As Mbembe predicts, such rage when unleashed proves uncontrollable and ultimately turns upon its own people in its drive for vengeance. Rage in BLM Gothic signifies a wound in the Black body through which monstrosity can infect. Of course, as suggested by the previous section, African Americans are not the originators of the illness but a victim of the infection.

Another form of monstrosity that appears in BLM Gothic texts is a controlled aggression which is nonetheless definitive of moral monstrosity. Like traditional monsters, the protagonists threaten normality with their violent but necessary

---

[180] LaValle, *Ballad*, p. 104. [181] LaValle, *Ballad*, p. 130. [182] LaValle, *Ballad*, p. 128.

eruptions. In keeping with Afropessimistic ethos, the protagonists reveal that normality itself is a nightmare that requires undoing as it destroys the humanity of both the anti-Black assailant(s)/cultures and the Black protagonist. Nia DaCosta's revisions to the Candyman mythos begun by Bernard Rose prove illustrative of this kind of controlled monstrosity. Unlike Rose's monster who mostly abides by the rules of his summoning, Da Costa's Candyman specifically targets perpetrators of anti-Blackness, rather than anyone who happens to be in the room or even his summoner. Consequently, the new Candyman kills an art curator and an art critic, both of whom exploited Black suffering for their own profit; a group of white teenaged girls who bully a Black teen; and, ultimately, the white officers who threaten Brianna, though Brianna was the one to summon Candyman.[183] In illustrating such choice and self-regulation in his inhuman violence, Da Costa's monster emphasizes his role as subverter of a horrifying normality.

Chris's fight to flee the Armitage house in *Get Out* perfectly illustrates this kind of controlled monstrosity. He utterly destroys the family, first stabbing Dean in the throat with the antlers of the mounted deer head before driving a pencil through Missy's eye; he then outwits Jeremy in a hand-to-hand fight before repeatedly stomping on his head. Finally, he confronts Rose, mounting her prone body to strangle her with his bare hands as the family's mansion burns in the background. Rose ceases pleading for her life and smiles as Chris's hands tighten around her throat, his face contorting with the effort and emotion (Figures 15 and 16). Her smile is telling and is similar to the narrative shift previously discussed in *The Ballad of Black Tom*; she seems to claim a victory as Chris, in the moment of brutality, is on the verge of confirming racist ideologies about Black violence and monstrosity. Chris can only respond by letting go, letting her live but also retaining a vestige of his humanity in order to disprove her racist presumptions.[184]

Rose's smile and the police threats to Brianna serve an important point in the iterations of Black turns to monstrosity. In placing them in the midst of scenes of profound Black violence, BLM Gothic points back to the originator of the illness. Jo's narrative arc in *Destroyer* exemplifies the ways the mode consistently dismantles reductions of Black radical violence to unfathomable monstrosity. A scientist, her rage puns on the trope of the 'mad' scientist in the Gothic tradition. In traditional Gothic literature and Horror film, the mad scientist is driven by an

---

[183] Burke recounts how Candyman murdered his sister as a child when she summoned him, thereby recalling the problematic behavior of the figure in Rose's film. The film explicitly addresses this incident as Burke emphasizes that the new Candyman will be imbued with a will to subvert racist structures and people.

[184] While some might argue that she smiles because she hears the approach of law enforcement, the smile comes well before the siren sounds.

Figure 15 Rose smiling as Chris strangles her

Figure 16 Chris's conflicted face just before he let's go of Rose's throat

illogical, (self-)destructive drive which is never fully explained. While Jo reproduces, to an extent, her ancestor Victor's madness, her drive for vengeance, power, and control of death is always couched in terms of her grief. Further, the series' consistent accounts of Jo's attempts to fight for progress through socially acceptable means only to continually confront systemic oppression clarify her determination to destroy the system that has tested her for too long. Her outlash signifies the '"cleansing" conditions of violence'[185] which Afropessimism defines as key for the Black theorist and Black theory if they are to truly disrupt systemic anti-Blackness and access full personhood.[186]

Although *Destroyer* initially opens with a depiction of Jo's mania, the series emphasizes how anti-Black culture cultivated her madness over the course of her life and finally triggered it when officers murder her twelve-year-old son, Akai. Volume three, for instance, features the scene in which Jo learns of Akai's murder. In the scene, Jo's skin grows grey and dark as she bends over weeping in front of an emotionless white officer. In the same volume, Jo briefly recounts the recent history of anti-Blackness, going back to Medgar Evan's murder and the acquittal of his murderer. She recalls Myrlie Evers, Medgar's wife, 'wishing she

---

[185] Wilderson III, *Red, White and Black*, p. 66.
[186] Wilderson's claim occurs in the context of debating the potential for Black film theory to destroy racially oppressive representational politics which also capture the Black film theorist: 'Black film theory, as an intervention, would have a more destructive impact if it foregrounded the impossibility of a Black film, the impossibility of a Black film theory, the impossibility of a Black film theorist, and the impossibility of a Black person except, and this is key, under the "cleansing" conditions of violence. Only when real violence is coupled with representational "monstrosity," can Blacks move from the status of things to the status of . . . of what, we'll just have to wait and see'. Wilderson, *Red, White and Black*, p. 66.

had a machine gun that night. If she had, she would've mowed down the police and her white neighbors. The depths of her hatred was indescribable'.[187] Volume five replays the scene leading to Akai's murder and volume six again recounts the entirety of the systemic assaults Jo suffers and connects them to Akai's murder by placing them amid a list of 'tests' Jo has endured. The last encounter is especially important as it occurs while Jo holds The Director's head, mourning that she did not get to kill the woman; it is also just before Jo attacks Pliers, Akai's father transformed into a machine.

Volume two elucidates the origin of her violent rage through its depictions of her cabin decorated her family photo collection, including pictures of Jo and Pliers happily embracing, and Akai as a baby, as a toddler, and as a twelve-year-old in his baseball uniform. The centre photo was taken, we later learn, before his baseball game on the day the police shot him. Although the series quickly marks Akai's death as the rupturing point, the collection of photos provide a more thorough overview of all Jo has been denied. The picture of Jo and Pliers suggests she has lost a lover and friend in Pliers; their relationship occupies a significant portion of one of the volumes. The photo of Jo applying a bandage to Akai reveals she has lost her place as a nurturer and the will to nurture. The numerous photos of Akai as an infant mark how precious he was to her and serve as a reminder of their shared innocence, something she also loses in his murder. Her cabin, which hides her lab, shows signs of the transformative loss that haunts because it perpetually threatens to return. Indeed, reflecting on Akai's murder, Jo mourns that she believed they were safe – she was a tenured professor living with Akai in a good neighbourhood where Akai attended private school. Ultimately, there is no safe place, a lesson which the series repeats in first the agents' breach followed by the Creature's invasion of Jo's fortified cabin home.

When placed into context even the excessiveness of her rage becomes not just fathomable but a logical response to an illogical, unending violence. The frequent compounding of so much pain, loss and suffering invites us to wonder that 'madness' is not more pervasive. Furthermore, these reminders of the long history of systemic, physical, and psychological violence Jo suffers are important as Jo puns on an anti-Black stereotype: the angry Black woman whose rage knows few bounds.[188] Iterations of this stereotype often imagine the figure as an emasculating hyper-bitch who even attacks members of her own family, especially men. To

---

[187] LaValle, *Destroyer* vol. 3.
[188] The text's dismantling of this stereotype is important given that the initial organizers for the BLM movement were three Black women. The stereotypes about Black functionally silence women, discouraging them from speaking out against their oppression and the oppression of their communities, and rendering their protests spectacles when they do dare to speak. See Collins, 'Mammies, Matriarchs and Other Controlling Images'.

African American Gothic 57

Figure 17 The Bride from James Whales's *The Bride of Frankenstein* (1935)

Figure 18 Jo in her lab coat

some extent, Jo's rage performs this stereotype in its unrestrained expression. Yet the graphic series forces us to keep her outburst in their psychosocial context. When she attacks Pliers, she reminds him and readers that he abandoned her in order to remain the servant of The Director. The first time she appears in her lab coat is after she has dreamed of Akai, a scene which ends with a nightmarish vision of him as talking corpse. The series visually marks Jo as a creation of white violence as her appearance recalls the depictions of the Bride in James Whale's *The Bride of Frankenstein* (1935) (Figure 17). Like Whale's Bride, Jo's hair is streaked white and she frequently appears in her white coat (Figure 18), her hands wearing a glove that easily replaces the original Bride's hand and wrist wrappings. Volume three emphasizes the connection in depicting Akai's last day alive. It shows Akai singing while getting dressed for his baseball game as Jo takes his picture; in the next panel Jo sits at the dinner table wondering why Akai is late returning home. The third frame is an extreme close-up of her face, her hair now streaked white and her eyes blazing green. Metaphorically, Jo's violence and rage are a form of the Bride's chaos-wreaking scream; both express female horror and pain. Both are also the creation of an uncontrolled, over-empowered whiteness which is ultimately the source of monstrosity. In commenting on Percy Shelley's edits to Mary Shelley's original text, LaValle alludes to this dynamic:

> Percy Shelley cut two vital details from Mary Shelley's original. In Mary's version the Creation pushes away from the ship. In Percy's he's simply pulled

away by the current. And in Mary's version Robert Walton's vision fails him, he loses sight of the creature. In Percy's version the Creation disappears.

. . . .

Only nine words separate the two, but Mary's version speaks a greater truth. It's the right of every Creation to reject a society that despises them. The responsibility of a just society is to truly see all of its Creations.[189]

The eruptions of radical violence in BLM Gothic must be read as this kind of rejection by a group that knows no other home.[190] In all of their raging, the protagonists in BLM Gothic reveal a need to subvert forced by the violence of a truly monstrous whiteness.

The texts disrupt temptations to accept the eruption of Black aggression as stereotypically monstrous by consistently placing it alongside iterations of oppressive white assaults to explain why the violence is necessary. For instance, the strange and wealthy recluse Suydam introduces Tommy to the Sleeping King in *The Ballad of Black Tom*. Seeking the aid of New York's disenfranchised racial and ethnic minorities, Suydam argues that waking the Sleeping King will dethrone their oppressors and allow them to institute a new world order. Yet Suydam's explanations about how and why he, a wealthy elite, came to be so concerned with the plight of the socially dispossessed amount to little more than an illogical rant. Upon closer inspection, Suydam yearns to bring about the world's destruction out of boredom and a thirst for more power, a quest which Black Tom ultimately subverts in his enraged drive for vengeance. Likewise, *Destroyer* begins not with Jo and Akai, but with images of Frankenstein's original Creature as a violent eco-warrior. Witnessing the slaughter of a whale by a ship, the Creature attacks the vessel before turning his attention to another ship nearby. Furthermore, the Creature's violence is extremely gruesome, as opposed to Jo's fairly clean and scientific assaults on the agents attacking her. Whereas Jo dissolves the agents' weapons, the Creature rips off arms and shatters skulls with his fists. While Jo's face becomes twisted in her rage, the Creature's face and body is literally soaked with gore. Notably, the captain of the second ship does not censure the Creature for his violence but rather offers to partner with it, arguing

---

[189] LaValle, *Destroyer* vol. 3, concluding comments.
[190] One could argue that BLM Gothic characters should follow the Creature's example and abandon the country, yet this too alludes back to a failed history of Black expatriation. Black artists of the mid twentieth century did, in fact, abandon the United States but this did not solve the problem of anti-Black violence on a large scale. Furthermore, there were several different attempts at large scale Black flight and deportation, from Marcus Garvey's attempt to facilitate Black migration to Liberia to Abraham Lincoln's failed trial at relocating free Blacks to Haiti. Black countries suffer from continued Imperialistic intrusions, and one might argue their history is illustrative of anti-Blackness on a global stage. More importantly, such movements invariably failed because they were premised on (accepting) the notion that Blacks had no right to or place in America.

'what you did wasn't futile. They killed those whales. Even the calf! Why should I feel anything for them?'[191] Unsurprisingly, the Creature kills everyone on that ship to, and the vessel crashes into a local harbour carrying the monster and a plethora of corpses.[192]

The captain's offer draws attention to the fact that the texts do not focus on single entries (or entities) of white villainy and monstrosity. In *Lovecraft Country* Atticus and friends must battle multiple iterations of white villainy, human and magical, from the Sons of Adam and their offshoots in the police force to entitled white heiresses to the ghosts of white scientists to very human gun-wielding and rape-threatening racists. Similarly, the ship captain is just the first of many iterations of human white villainy in *Destroyer*. Educating himself on the changes in the world since his departure, the Creature watches videos of soldiers in World War I dying from gas attacks and white police officers shooting a Black man in the back. A government-backed agency led by a white woman called only 'The Director' seeks to use him for their own purposes; this same agency is responsible for the attacks on Jo and the utter dehumanization of Pliers. All of these figures allude to a systemic anti-Blackness that inherently dehumanizes Blacks and renders them passive in the process. They are the modern iterations of the violence Jo recounts in historicizing her rage.

As much as these turns to monstrous violence are understandable and even justified, BLM Gothic warns that they come at a severe cost and mourns their necessity. The texts repeat the horrors detailed in Fanon's recount of the Algerian war, a racialized conflict that 'threatened to transform everyone, to varying degrees, into statues of hatred and empty them of all human feelings – pity, for starters – as well as the capacity to let oneself be touched, to recall one's own vulnerability to misfortune and to the distress of Others'.[193] In other words, the turn to the monstrous even in acts of controlled, radical violence also means 'The eradicating of all feelings of pity'.[194] This loss of pity, vulnerability, and humanity proves difficult to contain and spreads from the dynamic between oppressors and oppressed to affect the relationships among the oppressed themselves. Burke's mission in *Candyman* perfectly exemplifies this danger. Suffering survivor's guilt multiple times over – triggered by his role in Sherman's murder – Burke's anger over the necropolitical ruin and stagnation of his community blinds him to Anthony's humanity, agency and right to life. The horror of Burke's blindness manifests in his speech about his plan. He explains 'I knew it was only a matter of time before the baby came back

---

[191] LaValle, *Destroyer* vol. 1.
[192] LaValle puns on *Dracula* with this scene; one could even argue that the captain offers to play Renfield to the Creature.
[193] Mbembe, *Necropolitics*, pp. 128–129.   [194] Mbembe, *Necropolitics*, p. 129.

here',[195] thereby emphasizing Anthony's innocence and vulnerability. Burke points to the violation of infants and innocents three times over in the exchange: he begins by noting the church they stand in is where he was baptized as a young child; he then lists 'their [white] babies' among Candyman's new targets; and he finally names Anthony 'the baby'. The repetition points to his utter loss of humanity as he gleefully embraces infanticide as part of his revenge. Equally important, Burke proves utterly oblivious to Anthony's suffering, cutting off his hand without any anaesthetic before forcing a hook into the bleeding stump. Likewise, he forces Brianna to witness the assault while ignoring her screams and pleas for mercy. In his enraged pursuit of retribution, Burke destroys a Black life, denying it basic recognition, and ignores the emotional pain of another, which he also places in danger.

In opening with the Creature's fight against various aggressors, *Destroyer*'s first two volumes serve as similar warnings. Turning to violence as a means to liberate himself and others, he also repeatedly destroys the very people he means to protect and eventually becomes numb to their vulnerability. For example, volume two opens with the Creature's history, starting in Ireland in 1799 where he encounters armed men. Raising his hands and asking for help, the men open fire on him, declaring 'Come see what men can do!'[196] The volume then jumps forward 200 years to Mexico, where the Creature joins a group of immigrants hoping to cross the US-Mexico wall. The first immigrant to address him is a child who speaks to his dead mother, declaring they are saved when the Creature joins them. Reaching the wall, the Creature pulls it down without regard for the immigrants, killing them in the process. The boy tries to stop him, repeating the Creature's words to the Irishmen: 'Please! Wait! I just need hel-'.[197] The mirroring between the two episodes marks the Creature as one among oppressed multitudes; nevertheless, in his monstrous rage, he becomes insensitive to the plights and pain of those who suffer like him.

Black Tom mourns his transformation and the consequent innocent victims his rage claims. Having awakened the Sleeping King and defeated Malone, Black Tom returns to his friend at the Victoria Society:

> Black Tom said, "I did something big, bigger than anyone will understand for a long time. I was just so angry."
>
> . . . .
>
> I was a good man, right? I mean I wasn't like my father, but I never did people wrong. Not truly.

---

[195] *Candyman* (2021).

[196] LaValle, *Destroyer* vol. 2. Notably, the Creature's raised hands repeats the 'hands-up, don't shoot' positioning of BLM protestors.

[197] LaValle, *Destroyer* vol. 2.

"No, you didn't," Buckeye said, looking his old friend directly in the eye. "You were always good people. Still are."

Black Tom smiled faintly but shook his head. "Every time I was around them, they acted like I was a monster. So I said goddamnit, I'll be the worst monster you ever saw!"

Newly arrived diners at nearby tables turned to look at Black Tom, but neither he nor Buckeye noticed.

"But I forgot," Black Tom said quietly. "I forgot about all this."

Black Tom scanned the tables of men and women dining at the Victoria Society. He pointed to the row of windows that opened onto 137th Street.

"Nobody here ever called me a monster," Black Tom said.[198]

In the exchange, Black Tom reveals that embracing monstrosity proves isolating and blinding, leading the justice warrior to overlook the very innocent people (who will be) caught in the crossfire. Failure to retain connection to those who reminded Tommy of his and their humanity ultimately leads to an utter loss of it. As Black Tom notes, when you become so overwhelmed by the violence of being called 'monster', you risk becoming a nightmare and destroyer to all around you, not just your intended targets. Further, in 'forgetting about' everything besides the racist aggressor and their evils, Black Tom unintentionally repeats the destructive disregard that anti-Blackness at best shows to its targets, reproducing the same end-result: a failure to recognize their subjectivity and the consequent murder of innocents.

Like Black Tom, protagonists who embrace monstrous radical violence risk reproducing the end results of the anti-Black violators they seek to thwart. In pursuing vengeance against white American oppressors, Black Tom not only fulfils Sudyam's mission but also eradicates Black existence. He consequently engages in the ultimate act of anti-Blackness. In his rage, Black Tom unwittingly becomes a tool of oppression and is arguably controlled by someone/something else. The Creature in *Destroyer* reveals a similar lesson in the repetition between his encounters in Ireland and at the US-Mexico border. While the Irishmen level their guns at him, inviting him to witness the power of men, US self-appointed patrolmen meet him at the border, guns similarly leveled at the immigrants. However, seeing that the Creature has done their work for them, the guards do not fire upon him but instead invite him to join them. The repetitions and shifts mark how the Creature has unwittingly integrated the violent lessons he learned in his first vulnerable moments and, like Black Tom, become the tool of violent oppressors.

Burke, likewise, becomes the tool of whiteness even as he hopes to raise another Candyman to fight it. Similar to the white curator and art critic who

---

[198] LaValle, *Ballad*, pp. 146–147.

sought to consume Anthony's pain for profit, Burke augments Anthony's pain for his own use. He dehumanizes Anthony in his determination to literally turn Anthony into a monster. To complete Anthony's transformation, Burke calls police officers and mimics the voice of a white person, crying 'Hello, yes! I think I saw the guy you're looking for, the Say My Name Killer. He's roaming around the rowhouses at Cabrini … uhh a Black man … ..around thirty. He's waving a hook and talking crazy. He's killing people down there'.[199] Like the woman who calls the officers on Akai in *Destroyer*, Burke weaponizes the police, targeting them at an innocent Black person, as he explicitly notes: 'Here we have the story of Anthony McKoy, artist who lost his mind, and the cops showed up and shot him down in cold blood without even saying a word'. His maniacal giggle at the end of the line signals both madness and joy, but it is a joy that fails to acknowledge how he is reproducing the very violence he rages against.

In some ways, the anxieties represented by the violent protagonists reflect an Afropessimistic rejection of the 'human' given the category is racially coded and biologically predetermined. If the 'human' is both the social and genetic inheritance of whiteness, then, as Section 2 notes, human(ity) is always inherently abhuman. This produces a particularly complicated inheritance for African Americans, many of whom are the social, and perhaps biological, descendants of whiteness. Figures like Tom and Burke demonstrate the disastrous inheritance borne out of existence within white supremacy; the subjects of disdain and exile, they nonetheless inherit and reproduce the behaviours of (ab)human whiteness.

Ultimately, the characters suffer a diminishing, if not utter loss, of humanity during their transformation even as the fight to force recognition of Black humanity is at the heart of their struggle. For instance, Jo's 'monstrous' creation reiterates Black humanity in the very moment of his resurrection; the first part of Akai which Jo manages to bring back is his heart. Yet this is also the part she repeatedly seeks to stifle, chastising him for being 'too tender-hearted'. Similarly, in *Lovecraft Country* Dee also stifles her heart and humanity at the conclusion. At only twelve-years old, Dee responds to Christina's pleas for help and mercy with shocking brutality. Utterly emotionless, Dee comments 'You still haven't learned' before violently snapping Christina's neck with such force that blood spurts from the woman. That Dee has been transformed into a monster out of nightmares becomes unmissable as the dominant sound in the moment stems from Dee's mechanical arm. Indeed, before killing Christina, Dee reveals her transformation by casting off her jacket to showcase the new arm in a way reminiscent of the *Terminator* films from the 1980s through early 2000s. The series' call-back to the other film franchise marks Dee as having

---

[199] *Candyman* (2021).

African American Gothic

Figure 19 Dee, after killing Christina in *Lovecraft Country*

undergone a transformation that is the reverse of the Terminators. While over the course of several films, the Terminator becomes increasingly human, eventually sacrificing himself to protect humanity, Dee's new arm marks her as shifting towards the abhuman even as she too transforms in order to protect (Black) humanity.

The staging of the scene likewise emphasizes Dee's transformation into something horrible. The encounter occurs at night with a full moon in the background amidst the ruins of a formerly castle-like mansion. As Dee approaches, the music shifts to an ominous tone reminiscent of monster movies from the mid twentieth century. After killing Christina, Dee looks up at the full moon; a Cthulhu creature in the backdrop looks up at the same time and unleashes a roar (Figure 19). The full moon and mirrored gestures between Dee and the Cthulhu imply that Dee is transforming into a creature too, and the Cthulhu vocalizes for Dee. Yet the scene also marks her age as her pigtails remind us of the absoluteness of the horror. Not only has she lost her humanity, but she has lost it as an innocent child. In Dee, we see the fullest warning and tragedy of the fight against anti-Blackness and the need to embrace radical violence.

Thus the greatest danger that comes with embracing monstrosity is the danger to the self. In each of the previously mentioned instances, the characters betray their intentions and become the very thing they despise. They ultimately lose themselves in the struggle and become a threat to everyone, anti-Black oppressors and Black innocents. This loss of control signals a shift towards a monstrosity that loses its radical elements; the eradication of pity and recognition in the protagonists also shifts them towards the realm of the unfathomable. Yet in each case, monstrous violence begins as the kind of 'regenerative violence' Fanon embraces and which Mbembe worries over. The endings also challenge the 'willfulness' in Wilson's theory of 'willful monstrosity,' which Dawn Keetley also reads as central to 'progressive horror':

> There is a strand of horror, however, in which (marginalized) protagonists consciously embrace the role of monster for themselves. In these texts, the values associated with both "normality" and the "monster" are flipped: the self-aware monster-hero revels in threatening the representatives of normality, now aligned as antagonistic, even expressly corrupt. Narratives of the voluntary monster ... invite more or less wholehearted audience identification with the monster. ... the "other" embraces their difference and fights back against the social structure that defined them as other in the first place.[200]

The turn to monstrosity in BLM Gothic texts is necessitated rather than chosen, and their embrace proves a point of horror. While figures like Black Tom certainly revel in tormenting the perpetrators of anti-Blackness, they also become truly monstrous in their failure to recognize their casualties. BLM Gothic texts ask us to identify with them – with their rage and their pain – but also warn us of utterly becoming consumed by that rage, of too eagerly embracing the monstrous, not because you unwittingly mark the boundaries of normality in embracing monstrosity,[201] but because of how you may reproduce the end results of the oppressive norm you rage against. If normality is the monster of the twenty-first century,[202] then becoming its blind tool is the true nightmare.

Destroyer and *Candyman* do offer some possibility for humane resistance amid horrific anti-Blackness. Significantly, volume one of *Destroyer* suggests that Jo's successful attempt to resurrect Akai is one of many that have failed previously. That the heart is at the centre of Jo's successful attempt serves to emphasize that the heart needs to remain at the centre of the fight against anti-Blackness. Consequently, Akai tries to modulate Jo's rage throughout the series. In combatting the invading agents, Akai dismantles their guns rather than killing them. In general, Akai hesitates to do any physical harm to a living creature and intervenes when Jo threatens to kill people. He signifies the revolutionary potential inherent in Mbembe's description of ravaged Black humanity 'As a human whose name is disdained, whose power of descent and generation has been foiled, whose face is disfigured, and whose work is stolen, he bears witness to a mutilated humanity, one deeply scarred by iron and

---

[200] Keetley, 'Monsters', p. 190.
[201] Keetley notes that 'While willful monsters elicit sympathy, even identification ... of the monster still threatens (and thus constitutes) "normality"'. 'Monsters', p. 190.
[202] Keetley, 'Monsters', p. 191.

alienation'.²⁰³ Yet he retains 'the possibilities for radical insurgency ... that are never fully annihilated' through his very damnation.²⁰⁴ While Mbembe's comment invites an Afropessimist reading, alluding to the world-ending violence of the slave revolt, Akai's body and behaviour suggest another option: a rejection of the human as the inheritance of white abhumanism in favour of a different way of being, a sort of metahumanity. Unlike traditional constructions which accept the possessions and destruction of the 'animal' by the 'human', Akai ultimately insists that all life is valuable, even the life of those who would hurt him.

More ambivalently, *Candyman* appears at the end of the film, having saved Brianna, and instructs her to tell everyone. However, he does not explain what she should tell them. In telling the story of his creation, Brianna may remind listeners of the nightmare that comes from anti-Blackness and the need to fight it. Or she may tell the story of his just vengeance. Similarly, although *Destroyer* seems to end on a hopeful note, with Akai smiling, and watching a baseball game in a stadium, he is isolated in his enjoyment. In both cases, the texts end in a truly Gothic space with an utterly open ending, as we cannot know what the next battle will bring: metahumanistic counterassaults to anti-Blackness or a fuller descent into monstrosity. The true nightmare of BLM Gothic is that in a society in the business of making monsters, (inherited) monstrosity might be inescapable.

Conclusion: When Tomorrow Comes

> I do think that more and more white people are recognizing that the actual structures are no longer functional and they're damaging our country. .... An increasing number of white people do recognize that the path we're on is unsustainable. Now whether that's going to be actually enough ... to actually turn the tide and actually have real changes, I vacillate back and forth about being optimistic and pessimistic.²⁰⁵

> In America, it is traditional to destroy the black body – it is heritage.²⁰⁶

> "You are saved" .... "What has cast such a shadow upon you?" "The Negro."²⁰⁷

In the 2019 *Twilight Zone* episode 'Replay', a Black single mother named Nina faces a normal but seemingly impossible task: delivering her son Dorian to his university campus. The episode opens with the two of them bantering over lunch in a diner; in the background, a white officer enters the establishment. Watching as a Black woman, mother, and aunt, my heart dropped as soon as the officer entered the scene. I groaned when Dorian accidentally squirts ketchup on

---

²⁰³ Mbembe, *Critique*, p. 36.   ²⁰⁴ Mbembe, *Critique*, p. 36.
²⁰⁵ Meraji, 'Payback's A B****'.   ²⁰⁶ Coates, *Between the World and Me*, p. 103.
²⁰⁷ Melville, 'Benito Cereno'.
    LaValle, *Ballad*, p. 139.

his chest, staining his white shirt red just at his heart. I knew what the stain signified and sat in tense horror watching the episode's events unfold. Nina owns a magic camcorder; every time she hits the rewind button, she travels back in time. The device proves truly indispensable as the white officer, Lasky, arrives to harass them with each new replay of events, no matter what Nina and Dorian do differently. In one of the attempts, Nina takes the offence and tries to subdue Lasky by approaching him at the diner, buying him a slice of apple pie and conversing with him in an attempt to remind him of their shared humanity. Of course, this too fails. On her fifth attempt, Nina reveals her experiences to Dorian, explaining that she needs his help. Dorian suggests that they take the one route she has yet to try – the road to her familial home. With the help of her brother Neil, they finally manage to get Dorian to school. Yet even there Lasky confronts them.

I turn to this episode because it exemplifies many of the tropes and patterns of BLM Gothic. A lone mother and son travel through an average US countryside on an average road on an unexceptional mission. There is nothing truly supernatural in the episode aside from Nina's ability to rewind time. The sheriff is not superhuman but he is a monster, his dropping lips and sneering face eliciting shudders each time he confronts the pair. Indeed, on the fifth rewind, as Nina and Dorian flee the diner to avoid encountering Lasky, the episode subtly draws upon Horror tropes when Nina runs into him at the door. She stops, and looks aghast as if beholding a monster in its human form; meanwhile, Lasky's face grotesquely fills much of the frame and his smile produces shivers. Explaining the situation to her brother Neil, Nina cries

> There's this cop. I've tried everything but he just keeps pulling us over again and again and again no matter what route we take, no matter how nice or how mean we are. He's always there. There's nothing I can do. We can't get past him. He always shows up. He's always on the verge of killing Dorian.[208]

Lasky may be human but he also has powers that extend from his racial privilege, augmented by his official position.[209] The extent of the anti-Black violence and harassment are quite typical, as Neil notes, explaining 'They always come'.[210] If Lasky seems to be everywhere, seems to always find them, it is because he is everywhere in a way. Lasky's uniform and position

---

[208] *Twilight Zone*, 'Replay'.
[209] The film short *Two Distant Strangers* (2020) follows a similar plot as Carter is trapped in a loop that always ends with Officer Merk murdering him. Like Nina, Carter tries various tactics to escape Merk's violent assault. However, whereas Lasky's monstrosity is utterly human, Merk is eventually revealed as superhuman in his monstrosity.
[210] *Twilight Zone*, 'Replay'.

mark him as part of a larger systemic monstrosity, an issue reiterated when several other police arrive at the university to confront the Black family.

The series reminds us that this era of anti-Blackness is neither new nor unusual for the nation. Arriving at Nina's familial home – a welcoming house in a warm neighbourhood – Nina explains that she never returned because 'my older brothers lost their lives here. Your uncle was shot a block over there. To me there were only two ways out of here: walking out and never looking back, or dead'.[211] Yet in its placelessness – set nowhere in particular, the story could take place anywhere in America – the episode, like the rest of BLM Gothic, reminds us that the neighbourhood is not the problem. Like Jo in *Destroyer*, Brianna in *Candyman* and, to some extent, Darryl in 'Haint in the Window', Nina presumes her success and disconnection from her past will protect her and Dorian. Where Jo is a brilliant scientist, Nina is a brilliant lawyer who wins all of her cases. As she explains to Lasky, she worked hard to earn her car, to get her son into college, and to assure his future. But none of this is capable of dissuading, much less stopping, Lasky and others like him. They are always going to come.

And this is perhaps the supreme horror of the episode and of BLM Gothic: the extent to which anti-Black violence has been normalized such that it seems the inescapable future of the country and its citizens. Unaware that Nina has been replaying their past and aiming for a different outcome – one which leads to the future she glimpses after suffering yet another violent attack – Dorian quips 'It's not all random though. .... Since the big bang set everything in motion everything that happens in this universe has to be the way it is. ... It's all just particles unfolding the way they're destined to. .... Things happen but they happen the way they should'.[212] The comment is tormenting and Nina of course refuses to accept the idea. The show hints that there might be different outcomes, but the different ones might actually be worse. The first few encounters Lasky pulls out his taser; on the fourth and fifth times, he pulls out his gun.

Unlike Afropessimistic BLM Gothic texts, 'Replay' eschews the turn to violent monstrosity. While Nina does grow enraged, screaming at Lasky in the restaurant parking lot on one attempt, and confronting him with her camera on the final attempt, she does not counter his violence with violence of her own. Rather she acknowledges Neil's challenge and critique to her when he asks 'The question is what are we gonna do? At least this time, there is a "we", and not just you and your boy. .... Ain't nothin' good ever come about in this country without us getting together'.[213] The episode signals this as the ideal resolution, presented in a room bathed in golden light and decorated with posters from

---

[211] *Twilight Zone*, 'Replay'.   [212] *Twilight Zone*, 'Replay'.   [213] *Twilight Zone*, 'Replay'.

previous eras of Black Rights struggles, Black Power fists, and BLM signs. The solution, the episode hopes, is in communal knowledge and resistance. Neil proposes to get Dorian to college using little-known side streets, back alleyways, and old drainage systems that he learned about while doing a remembrance project to counter the erasure that gentrification threatens. Their unified effort proves successful. Even though Lasky confronts them on the campus, another communal effort saves the group as the collection of Black parents and children follow Nina's lead and raise their camera phones to record the officers. Nina's monologue provides a useful commentary as it also gestures back to the violent solutions found in Afropessimistic BLM Gothic texts:

> You've crossed the line. Harassing us, abusing authority; you've been profiling us, targeting us, following us, shooting us, killing us. [shaking her head] Uh uh not anymore, now we cross the line. My son will cross that gate right, now right here. My son will go to college. So back the fuck up. . . . . I see it now, Officer Lasky. You're the one who's really afraid.[214]

Like LaValle's comments in *Destroyer*, Nina's speech reveals that fear of Black empowerment fuels Lasky's monstrosity. Like the other texts, Dorian will cross a line; the difference is that he will cross into power through becoming a successful filmmaker – his chosen major and career – rather than embracing monstrosity.

As much as BLM Gothic is concerned with the violence and horrors targeted at Black Americans, it also stresses how systemic anti-Blackness is a curse that impacts whiteness as well.[215] While *Lovecraft Country* stresses the profound evils Blacks suffer from white assault, the series also reveals the intraracial oppression occurring among white Americans. This is most apparent in Christina's narrative arc, as she is the one to sabotage her father's initial ritual and free Atticus. She decries the gendered subjugation and exclusion she suffers at the hands of other white men; thus while Ruby chooses to explore life as a white woman, thereby accessing the privileges denied her as a Black person, Christina chooses the body of a white man for her alter-ego.

Ghost Boys also explores the impact anti-Blackness has on white Americans through Sarah, the daughter of the officer who shoots Jerome. Sarah is a lonely girl and quickly becomes friends with ghost Jerome, who poignantly notes 'Die, and a white girl can be your friend'.[216] Although Jerome stresses how Black

---

[214] *Twilight Zone*, 'Replay'.
[215] BLM Gothic performs the kind of intersectionality that Black feminists like Audre Lorde argue as integral to understanding and dismantling oppression(s). In 'Age, Race, Class and Sex: Women Redefining Difference' Lorde emphasizes the ways in which seemingly disparate oppressions ultimately articulate the same ideology and methodology against different populations.
[216] Rhodes, *Ghost Boys*, p. 67.

children are denied friendship with white children, Sarah's pleading with him to stay reveals that she too – and other children like her – suffer from the de facto segregation. Furthermore, the novel emphasizes the familial costs of Officer Moore's actions: Sarah spends hours on her computer, rarely leaving her room and isolating herself from friends, while 'her dad drinks, [and] stares at the TV' and 'Her mom sleeps the days away in bed'.[217] Moore's family, secure in its economic and racial privileges, nevertheless suffer a ruination and pain similar to Jerome's family. BLM Gothic hopes to awaken white Americans to the horrors of the oppression they perpetuate by reminding them of the subtle ways it slowly destroys them. Neil's comment 'Ain't nothin' good ever come about in this country without us getting together'[218] therefore might be taken more radically and in a larger context. 'Us' might not just be limited to African Americans; 'us' might include the many other Americans who suffer under a system that thrives off of disenfranchising portions of its population. Indeed, in marking a disembodied/unseen agent as a governing force of whiteness, texts like 'Everybody Dies!' and *Destroyer* exemplify the notion of biological whiteness as an inheritance of a social and environmental system regulating the expression of genetic inheritance. Whiteness does not have to express its monstrous inheritance. Though we may be 'affected by the social and environmental experiences of our recent ancestors' we can also reverse them and turn off the monstrous inheritance 'precisely because they rely upon social and environmental cues'.[219]

BLM Gothic texts rarely have closed endings. The protagonists may survive, but to what end? *Lovecraft Country* ends on a seemingly victorious note, as Leti defeats Christina proclaiming 'magic is ours now',[220] yet we never see what kind of tomorrow that claim produces. Tommy/ Black Tom notes that things are going to (violently) change but when is impossible to know. Nor does the text predict what exactly that change will actually look like. Indeed officer Malone, now traumatized and physically scarred from his encounter with Black Tom, reproduces the conclusion to Melville's story of another Black revolt against violent white subjugation. Though his therapist insists that Blacks' 'simplicity was their gift, and their curse',[221] Malone has been forced to see what his therapist and the rest of society will not: they live in 'a universe in which all the powers of the NYPD could not defeat a single Negro with a razor blade'.[222] Like Cereno, Malone cannot un-see the truth of the world he lives in; Tom removes Malone's eyelids to make sure Malone can never shut his eyes to the horrors of anti-Blackness again or to the power of Blacks to destroy worlds.

---

[217] Rhodes, *Ghost Boys*, p. 179.   [218] *Twilight Zone*, 'Replay'.
[219] Jackson, *Becoming Human*, p. 200.   [220] 'Full Circle' ep. 10, *Lovecraft Country*.
[221] LaValle, *Ballad*, p. 139.   [222] LaValle, *Ballad*, p. 139.

Brian Danoff's reading of the conclusion of 'Benito Cereno' proves true for *The Ballad of Black Tom* as well: though the status quo might have been temporarily restored, 'as long as the institution of slavery persists, more trouble is looming on the horizon'.[223] BLM Gothic narratives may take place in the era long after slavery's end, but its Afropessimist leanings remind us that 'the black subject in Western society is synonymous with ... Slave'.[224] BLM Gothic warns that until we actually change our structural and ideological patterns, there is more horror to come for all of us.

The most hopeful ending among the texts appears in *Destroyer*. Having died from being seen as a monster when a living child, Akai claims some of the power of monstrosity for himself in his afterlife. Thus when Jo warns him that some people will fear him, Akai responds 'I think they already do'.[225] While the comment clearly has tragic resonances, given the details of Akai's murder, Akai also presents it as a point of empowerment, smiling and flexing his muscles as he says it. After the death of his mother, Akai learns about Black disenfranchisement and the repressed history of Black power and accomplishment. The final panels of the series offer a hopeful sign. The first features Akai sitting among the bleachers at a baseball field, a look of joy on his face. The final panel is a close-up of a foam finger painted number one; the finger points above to Akai. The two panels seemingly indicate a victory for Akai and Jo. They also suggest a new beginning as Akai is the first of his kind, signifying a metahumanity borne as an inherited Black resistance to white abhumanity.[226] Yet, given Jo's warnings, the extent of this victory and the nature of what comes after this new beginning proves uncertain.

Importantly 'Replay' points to art as a form of power multiple times over, thereby reminding us of the power of stories and their tellers to effect change. Lasky reacts with terrible rage each time he sees Nina's camcorder; in the final confrontation, a brief shot presents Nina's camcorder as the counter weapon to Lasky's gun as the barrels of each is pointed at the other. We might, therefore, look at BLM Gothic as a kind of weapon, aimed at ending the long, systemic history of anti-Blackness. That art might serve as such a weapon is perhaps apparent in the fact the Rhodes's book *Ghost Boys* has been banned in at least one California school district. Maybe art can get us to a warm, sunlit future. The

---

[223] Danoff, 'I'm the Captain Now', p. 47.
[224] Jenkins, 'Afro-Futurism/Afro-Pessimism', p. 126. [225] LaValle, *Destroyer* vol. 5.
[226] Although we can argue the Creature as a kind of ancestor for Akai, the two are different in important ways. Their creations differ, they have different powers – the Creature uses brute force while Akai uses technology similar to nanobots – and, most importantly, they have a different relationship to their creators.

final scene of 'Replay' takes place ten years later in the future Nina previously glimpsed.

Of the various texts covered in this discussion, the one that has a certain end is 'Everybody Dies!' There, despite all her efforts to escape and end her role in the cycle of Black death, Rippa the Reaper remains trapped on the stage, tears streaming from her eyes, as she sings the theme song for the show. What is certain, the film short concludes, is that there is more Black suffering, pain, and loss to come for the foreseeable future. Alas, even 'Replay' acknowledges this heart-rending truth, revealing that any prospective hope is already circumscribed as future happiness, tranquility, and peace always have a timer on it. Nina's granddaughter accidentally breaks the camcorder and Dorian comforts his mother, telling her it is time to let it go. Smiling, he leaves to get them ice cream as the voice-over narration begins. The camera frames Nina's face, her smile slowly falling away as Jordan Peele's voice proclaims 'It was love, not magic, that kept evil at bay. But for some evils, there are no magical, permanent solutions'.[227] As he speaks, red and blue flashing lights are subtly reflected on Nina's face, eerie music begins to pick up in volume and Peele, like the BLM Gothic, concludes 'the future remains uncertain'.[228] We might make it through years of tomorrows, but anti-Black violence will still claim its victims eventually in America's necropolitical landscape. 'Replay' exemplifies the hope and despair of the BLM movement in its arc, and the nightmarish, Afropessimistic model of BLM Gothic in its ending. The lesson of its conclusion, much like the lesson of history to BLM activists, is to 'stay woke', camera ever at the ready. It is a reality born out of horror: Stay awake, lest you die in your sleep.

---

[227] *Twilight Zone*, 'Replay'.   [228] *Twilight Zone*, 'Replay'.

Bibliography

American Gods, 'The Secret of Spoons', Amazon Prime, 7 May 2017, series.

Arendt, Hannah, *Eichmann in Jerusalem: A Report on the Banality of Evil* (London: Penguin, 2006).

Barnes, Rodney, 'The Goatman', *Run, Fool!* (Ballen Studios), 9 January 2024. https://player.fm/series/3528461/394236883 [last accessed 18 January 2024].

Benson-Allott, Caetlin, 'Learning from Horror', *Film Quarterly* 70.2 (Winter 2016): 58–62.

Bouie, Jamelle, 'Michael Brown Wasn't a Superhuman Demon', *Slate*, 26 November 2014.

https://slate.com/news-and-politics/2014/11/darren-wilsons-racial-portrayal-of-michael-brown-as-a-superhuman-demon-the-ferguson-police-officers-account-is-a-common-projection-of-racial-fears.html [last accessed 9 June 2023].

'A Breakdown of Lovecraft Country's Costumes', *ENews*, 3 February 2021. www.eonline.com/photos/31529/a-breakdown-of-lovecraft-countrys-costumes [last accessed 18 September 2023].

Candyman, Nia DaCosta (director and writer), DVD (2021).

Coates, Ta-Nehisi, *Between the World and Me* (Melbourne: Text, 2015).

Collins, Patricia Hill (ed.), 'Mammies, Matriarchs and Other Controlling Images', in *Black Feminist Thought: Knowledge, Consciousness, and the Politics of Empowerment* (London: Routledge, 2000), pp. 69–96.

Danoff, Brian, '"I'm the Captain Now": Power, Justice, and Tragedy in "Benito Cereno" and Captain Phillips', *American Political Thought* 6.1 (Winter 2017): 30–53.

Due, Tananarive (ed.), 'The Haint in the Window', in *The Wishing Pool: And Other Stories* (New York: Akashic Books, 2023), pp. 32–49.

Dyer, Richard, *White: The Twentieth Anniversary Edition* (London: Taylor and Francis, 2017).

Eligon, John, 'The Quiet Casualties of the Movement for Black Lives', *The New York Times*, 28 March 2018. www.nytimes.com/2018/03/28/insider/black-lives-matter-stress.html [last accessed 22 July 2024].

'Everybody Dies!' Nuotama Bodomo (writer, director) in *Collective: Unconscious* (2016).

Fanon, Frantz, *The Wretched of the Earth* (New York: Grove Press, 1963).

Fanon, Frantz, *Black Skin White Masks* (London: Pluto Press, 2008).

Giroux, Henry, 'Reading Hurricane Katrina: Race, Class, and the Biopolitics of Disposability', *College Literature* 33.3 (2006): 171–196.

Harrison, Sheri-Marie, 'New Black Gothic', *Los Angeles Review of Books*, 23 June 2018. https://lareviewofbooks.org/article/new-black-gothic/ [last accessed 31 January 2023].

Hitchens, Brooklyn K., 'Contextualizing Police Use of Force and Black Vulnerability: A Response to Whitesel', *Sociological Forum* 32.2 (June 2017): 434–438.

Hooks, Bell, *Black Looks: Race and Representation* (Boston, MA: South End Press, 1992).

Jackson, Zakiyyah Iman, *Becoming Human: Matter and Meaning in an Antiblack World* (New York: New York University Press, 2020).

Jenkins, Candice M., 'Afro-Futurism/ Afro-Pessimism', in Joshua Miller (ed.), *The Cambridge Companion to Twenty-First-Century American Literature* (Cambridge: Cambridge University Press, 2021), pp. 123–141 (p. 129).

Keetley, Dawn, 'Monsters and Monstrosity', in Stephen Shapiro and Mark Storey (eds.), *The Cambridge Companion to American Horror* (Cambridge: Cambridge University Press, 2022), pp. 183–197.

LaValle, Victor, *The Ballad of Black Tom* (New York: Tor.com, 2016).

LaValle, Victor, *Victor LaValle's Destroyer*, 6 vols (Los Angeles: Boom! Studios, 2017).

Lovecraft Country 10 episodes Misha Green (creator), HBO.

'Mamie Till Mobley', *American Experience*, PBS.com. www.pbs.org/wgbh/americanexperience/features/emmett-biography-mamie-till-mobley/ [last accessed 11 October 2023].

Mbembe, Achille, *Critique of Black Reason* (Durham: Duke University Press, 2017).

Mbembe, Achille, *Necropolitics* (Durham: Duke University Press, 2019).

Means Coleman, Robin R., *Horror Noire: Blacks in American Horror Film from the 1890s to the Present* (New York: Routledge, 2011).

Means Coleman, Robin R., and Novotny Lawrence, 'A Peaceful Place Denied: Horror Film "Whitopias"', in Dawn Keetley (ed.), *Jordan Peele's Get Out* (Columbus, OH: The Ohio State University Press, 2020), pp. 47–62.

Melville, Herman, 'Benito Cereno', in *The Piazza Tales* (New York: Dix & Edwards, 1856), pp. 109–270.

Meraji, Shereen Marisol, 'Payback's A B****', *Code Switch*, podcast audio, 26 February 2021. www.npr.org/2021/01/14/956822681/paybacks-a-b [last accessed 12 November 2023].

Mishra, Pankaj, 'Frantz Fanon's Enduring Legacy', *The New Yorker*, 21 November 2021. www.newyorker.com/magazine/2021/12/06/frantz-fanons-enduring-legacy [last accessed 17 January 2024].

Mittman, Asa, 'Introduction: The Impact of Monsters and Monster Studies', in Asa Simon Mittman and Peter J. Dendle (eds.), *The Ashgate Research Companion to Monsters and the Monstrous* (Farnham: Ashgate, 2012), pp. 1–14.

Page, Thomas Nelson, *The Negro: The Southerner's Problem* (New York: Scribner's Sons, 1904).

Park, Linette, 'Afropessimism and Futures of . . . : A Conversation with Frank Wilderson', *The Black Scholar* 50:3 (Fall 2020) pp. 29–41.

Rhodes, Jewell Parker, *Ghost Boys* (London: Orion Children's Books, 2018).

Solomon, Robert C., *In Defense of Sentimentality* (Oxford: Oxford University Press, 2004).

The American Experience, 'The Murder of Emmett Till', PBS, 27 August 2020, television broadcast. www.pbs.org/wgbh/americanexperience/films/till/ [last accessed 11 October 2023].

Twilight Zone, 'Replay', CBS, 11 April 2019, television series.

Washington, Glenn, 'Dismal Falls', *KQED & PRX: Snap Judgement Presents: Spooked*, podcast audio, 19 August 2022. https://spookedpodcast.org/ [last accessed 31 January 2024].

Washington, Glenn, 'The Intruders', *KQED & PRX: Snap Judgement Presents: Spooked*, podcast audio, 23 October 2018. https://spookedpodcast.org/ [last accessed 31 January 2024].

Weinstock, Jeffrey, 'Invisible Monsters: Vision, Horror, and Contemporary Culture', in Asa Simon Mittman and Peter J. Dendle (eds.), *The Ashgate Research Companion to Monsters and the Monstrous* (Surrey: Ashgate, 2013), pp. 275–289.

Wester, Maisha L., *African American Gothic: Screams from Shadowed Places* (New York: Palgrave Macmillan, 2012).

Wester, Maisha L., '"Nightmares of the Normative": African American Gothic and the Rejection of the American Ideal', in Sorcha Ni Fhlainn and Bernice Murphy (eds.), *Twentieth-Century Gothic* (Edinburg: Edinburgh University Press, 2022), pp. 273–279.

Wilderson III, Frank B., *Red, White and Black: Cinema and the Structure of US Antagonisms* (Durham: Duke University Press, 2010).

Wilson, Natalie, *Willful Monsters* (Jefferson, NC: McFarland, 2020).

Wright, Richard, 'The Ethics of Living Jim Crow: An Autobiographical Sketch', in Richard Wright (ed.), *Uncle Tom's Children* (New York: Harper Perennial, 1989), pp. 1–15.

Cambridge Elements

The Gothic

Dale Townshend
Manchester Metropolitan University
Dale Townshend is Professor of Gothic Literature in the Manchester Centre for Gothic Studies, Manchester Metropolitan University.

Angela Wright
University of Sheffield
Angela Wright is Professor of Romantic Literature in the School of English at the University of Sheffield and co-director of its Centre for the History of the Gothic.

Advisory Board
Enrique Ajuria Ibarra, *Universidad de las Américas, Puebla, Mexico*
Katarzyna Ancuta, *Chulalongkorn University, Thailand*
Fred Botting, *University of Kingston, UK*
Carol Margaret Davison, *University of Windsor, Ontario, Canada*
Rebecca Duncan, *Linnaeus University, Sweden*
Jerrold E. Hogle, *Emeritus, University of Arizona*
Mark Jancovich, *University of East Anglia, UK*
Dawn Keetley, *Lehigh University, USA*
Roger Luckhurst, *Birkbeck College, University of London, UK*
Eric Parisot, *Flinders University, Australia*
Andrew Smith, *University of Sheffield, UK*

About the Series
Seeking to publish short, research-led yet accessible studies of the foundational 'elements' within Gothic Studies as well as showcasing new and emergent lines of scholarly enquiry, this innovative series brings to a range of specialist and non-specialist readers some of the most exciting developments in recent Gothic scholarship.

Cambridge Elements

The Gothic

Elements in the Series

Gothic Voices: The Vococentric Soundworld of Gothic Writing
Matt Foley

Mary Robinson and the Gothic
Jerrold E. Hogle

Folk Gothic
Dawn Keetley

The Last Man and Gothic Sympathy
Michael Cameron

Democracy and the American Gothic
Michael J. Blouin

Dickens and the Gothic
Andrew Smith

Contemporary Body Horror
Xavier Aldana Reyes

The Music of the Gothic: 1789–1820
Emma McEvoy

The Eternal Wanderer: Christian Negotiations in the Gothic Mode
Mary Going

African American Gothic in the Era of Black Lives Matter
Maisha Wester

A full series listing is available at: www.cambridge.org/GOTH

For EU product safety concerns, contact us at Calle de José Abascal, 56–1°,
28003 Madrid, Spain or eugpsr@cambridge.org.

www.ingramcontent.com/pod-product-compliance
Ingram Content Group UK Ltd.
Pitfield, Milton Keynes, MK11 3LW, UK
UKHW022113130426
469895UK00013B/177